Welcome to Porto, a captivating city steeped in history, culture, and natural beauty. As the second largest city in Portugal, Porto offers a rich tapestry of experiences waiting to be discovered by the curious traveler. Our travel guide has been meticulously crafted to help you uncover the hidden gems, embrace the local customs, and immerse yourself in the vibrant atmosphere that makes Porto so unique.

From the iconic Dom Luís I Bridge to the charming streets of Ribeira, we've got you covered with our expert suggestions, insider tips, and carefully curated itineraries designed to make your trip truly unforgettable. This guide will walk you through the best sights, tastes, and sounds that Porto has to offer, while also providing practical information to ensure a seamless journey through the city.

Whether you're a first-time visitor or a seasoned traveler, our goal is to make your Porto experience as enriching and memorable as possible. So, pack your bags, lace up your walking shoes, and get ready to embark on an extraordinary adventure through the enchanting city of Porto. Let the journey begin!

# Contents

# 1. Introduction

Porto is one of Portugal's most historic and beautiful cities. Situated on the Douro River, Porto is known for its stunning views, its UNESCO World Heritage Site status, and its delicious port wine.

Porto's history dates back to the 4th century, when the city was founded by the Celts. In the 12th century, Porto became an important stop for ships travelling up and down the Douro River, and the city began to grow. By the 13th century, Porto was an important trading city, and in 1383, it was given the status of a city by King Ferdinand I.

Over the centuries, Porto has been ruled by the Moors, the Romans, and the Portuguese. Each group has left its mark on the city, and today, Porto is a fascinating mix of old and new.

The Old Town is a warren of narrow streets and alleyways, lined with traditional houses and shops. The New Town is a more modern area, with wide boulevards and grand buildings.

Between the Old and New Towns is the Ribeira district, which is one of the most beautiful parts of Porto. The Ribeira is home to the city's historic waterfront, as well as its many cafes, bars, and restaurants.

If you're looking for views, you can't go wrong with the Ponte Luis I. This bridge, which spans the Douro River, offers stunning views of the city, the river, and the surrounding countryside.

For something a little different, be sure to visit the Livraria Lello. This beautiful bookstore, which dates back to 1906, is one of the most photographed places in Porto. Its striking interior, with its ornate wooden shelves and stained glass skylight, is truly a sight to behold.

And of course, no visit to Porto would be complete without trying its famous port wine. Porto's port wine is world-renowned, and the city is home to many of the best port wine producers in the world. Whether you prefer your port red or white, dry or sweet, you're sure to find a style that you love.

So what are you waiting for? Come and explore Porto – a city that has something for everyone.

## 1.1 Why Visit Porto

Porto, the second-largest city in Portugal, is a captivating destination for travelers seeking a unique blend of history, culture, and modernity. With its stunning riverside setting, picturesque streets, and warm, welcoming atmosphere, Porto offers an unforgettable experience that will leave you longing for more. Here are some compelling reasons to visit this enchanting city:

1. Rich history and UNESCO World Heritage sites: Porto's historical center, Ribeira, is a UNESCO World Heritage site, showcasing a myriad of architectural styles and centuries-old monuments. The city's history dates back to Roman times, and its well-preserved buildings and structures offer a fascinating glimpse into its past.

2. Beautiful architecture: Porto is renowned for its diverse architectural styles, ranging from medieval to baroque, neoclassical, and modern. Iconic landmarks such as the Clérigos Tower, São Bento Railway Station, and Livraria Lello are just a few examples of Porto's architectural treasures.

3. World-famous wine: As the birthplace of port wine, Porto is a must-visit for wine enthusiasts. The Douro Valley, the region where port wine is produced, is just a short drive away, offering opportunities to tour wineries, attend tastings, and learn about the winemaking process.

4. Vibrant arts and culture scene: Porto's thriving arts scene includes contemporary art museums, galleries, and street art, along with traditional music and dance performances. The Serralves Foundation, the city's premier contemporary art institution, is a must-visit for art lovers.

5. Culinary delights: Porto's gastronomy is a blend of traditional Portuguese flavors and innovative cuisine. The city's food scene features everything from cozy taverns to Michelin-starred restaurants, offering dishes such as francesinha, bacalhau, and pastel de nata. The historic Bolhão Market is an excellent place to sample local produce and delicacies.

6. Stunning natural surroundings: Porto's location along the Douro River and proximity to the Atlantic Ocean provide opportunities for

outdoor enthusiasts to enjoy scenic walks, bike rides, and watersports. The city's coastal suburbs offer beautiful beaches, while the nearby Douro Valley and Peneda-Gerês National Park are perfect for hiking and exploring.

7.  Warm and welcoming people: The people of Porto, known as "Tripeiros," are known for their friendliness and hospitality. As a visitor, you'll feel warmly welcomed and embraced by the local community, making your stay in Porto even more enjoyable.

8.  Affordability: Porto is a relatively affordable European destination, offering excellent value for money. With reasonably priced accommodation, dining, and attractions, you can enjoy a memorable vacation without breaking the bank.

9.  Easy accessibility: Porto's well-connected international airport, efficient public transportation system, and walkable city center make it easy to explore the city and its surroundings. The city's compact size means that you can see many of its top sights in just a few days.

In summary, Porto is a captivating city that blends history, culture, and natural beauty, offering a memorable and enriching experience for travelers. Its warm and welcoming atmosphere, combined with its affordability and accessibility, make it an ideal destination for your next vacation.

## 1.2 A Brief History of Porto

Porto is a city in northern Portugal on the Douro River. It is the second-largest city in the country after Lisbon and has a population of about 1.3 million people. The city is known for its port wine, which is exported from the city's port. Porto is also a popular tourist destination.

The city of Porto was founded by the Celts in the 4th century BC. It was later conquered by the Romans, who named it Portus Cale. Under Roman rule, the city became an important trading center. In the 5th century, the city was conquered by the Visigoths. From the 8th to the 11th centuries, Porto was an important center of the Muslim Umayyad Caliphate.

In the 12th century, the city was conquered by the first King of Portugal, Afonso Henriques. The city became an important center of the Portuguese kingdom and was the capital of Portugal from 1383 to 1385.

In the 15th and 16th centuries, the city prospered due to the wine trade. The city's golden age came in the 18th century under the rule of Marquis of Pombal. Pombal made many improvements to the city, including the construction of new roads and bridges.

In the 19th century, the city grew rapidly due to industrialization. The city's port became one of the largest in Europe. In the 20th century, the city was damaged by two earthquakes, in 1917 and in 1957. The city was also affected by the Portuguese Colonial War (1961-1974).

Today, Porto is a major economic center in Portugal. The city's economy is based on tourism, trade, and industry. The city is home to many universities and research institutes.

## 1.3 Porto's Unique Culture and Identity

Porto is a city with a rich and unique culture and identity. Situated on the banks of the River Douro, Porto is steeped in history and has a distinctly different feel to other cities in Portugal. Porto is known for its medieval churches, its stunning architecture and its friendly, welcoming people.

The city has a strong maritime tradition and is home to some of the best port wine in the world. Porto is also a city of art and culture, with a vibrant music and arts scene. There are plenty of things to see and do in Porto, making it the perfect destination for a city break.

If you're looking to experience the real Porto, then head to the **Ribeira** district. This is the historic heart of the city and is where you'll find the best views of the River Douro. The Ribeira is also home to the city's iconic bridges, including the Dom Luis I bridge.

For a taste of the city's port wine, head to one of the many port wine lodges in the Vila Nova de Gaia district. Here you can learn about the history of port wine and taste some of the best varieties.

If you're looking for a more cultural experience, then be sure to visit the **Palacio de Bolsa**. This former stock exchange is now a museum that tells the story of Porto's commerce and trade.

And no visit to Porto would be complete without taking a ride on the iconic **yellow tram**. These trams have been carrying passengers around the city since 1895 and are a great way to see the sights.

So, whether you're looking to sample the city's port wine, marvel at its architecture or simply soak up the atmosphere, Porto has something for everyone.

# 2. Planning Your Trip

When planning your trip to Porto, there are a few things to take into account. Porto is a large city, and as such, it can be difficult to navigate. Be sure to map out your route in advance and give yourself plenty of time to explore.

Porto is also a very hilly city, so be prepared for some uphill walking. Wear comfortable shoes and pack a bottle of water.

If you're visiting Porto in the summer, be aware that it can be quite hot. Temperatures often exceed 30 degrees Celsius. Drink plenty of water and take breaks often to avoid heat exhaustion.

If you're visiting Porto on a budget, there are a few things you can do to save money. Many of the city's attractions are free, such as the Palacio de Bolsa and the Igreja de Santo Ildefonso. You can also find discounts on food and accommodation if you book in advance.

When packing for your trip, remember to pack comfortable clothes and shoes. Porto is a casual city, so there's no need to dress up.

## 2.1 Best Time to Visit Porto: Seasons, Weather, and Events

Porto, like the rest of Portugal, experiences a Mediterranean climate with mild, wet winters and warm, dry summers. To make the most of your trip, it's essential to understand the city's seasonal variations, as each offers unique experiences, weather conditions, and events.

High Season (June - August)

The high season in Porto falls during the summer months, from June to August. This period is characterized by warm and sunny weather, with average temperatures ranging from 60°F (16°C) to 75°F (24°C). Summer is an ideal time for outdoor activities, beach trips, and exploring the nearby Douro Valley.

During these months, the city buzzes with energy and hosts numerous events and festivals, such as São João Festival in June and NOS Primavera Sound music festival in July. However, the high season also brings larger crowds, higher accommodation prices, and increased waiting times at popular attractions.

Shoulder Season (April - May and September - October)

The shoulder season, comprising of spring (April-May) and autumn (September-October), offers a balance between pleasant weather and fewer crowds. Spring in Porto is characterized by mild temperatures, ranging from 52°F (11°C) to 66°F (19°C), and blooming flowers. Autumn, on the other hand, sees temperatures between 54°F (12°C) and 73°F (23°C) with beautiful fall foliage.

This period is ideal for sightseeing and outdoor activities, as the weather is still comfortable but less crowded than the high season. During the shoulder season, you can also enjoy events like Fantasporto, an international film festival held in late February to early March, and the Porto Marathon in November.

Low Season (November - March)

The low season in Porto falls during the winter months, from November to March. The city experiences mild temperatures, with averages between 44°F (7°C) and 57°F (14°C), and increased rainfall. While outdoor activities might be limited due to the weather, Porto's many indoor attractions, such as museums, galleries, and wine cellars, can still be enjoyed.

During the low season, you can experience Porto's Christmas festivities and the Essência do Vinho wine festival in February. This period also offers lower accommodation prices and fewer crowds, providing a more relaxed and budget-friendly experience.

In conclusion, the best time to visit Porto depends on your preferences and priorities. For warm weather, outdoor activities, and lively events, visit during the high season. If you prefer milder temperatures and fewer crowds, opt for the shoulder season. For budget-conscious travelers who don't mind the cooler weather and rain, the low season is a suitable option.

## 2.2 Getting to Porto

Porto is well-connected and easily accessible from various locations, both internationally and within Portugal. Here are several transportation options to help you plan your journey to Porto:

**By Air:**

Francisco Sá Carneiro Airport (OPO) is Porto's main international airport, located approximately 11 kilometers (7 miles) northwest of the city center. It serves numerous airlines, including major carriers and low-cost options, with flights from cities across Europe, North America, and other destinations.

To search for flights and compare prices, you can use websites like Skyscanner (https://www.skyscanner.com/), Google Flights (https://www.google.com/flights), and Kayak (https://www.kayak.com/).

From the airport, you can reach the city center by various means:

1. Metro: The airport is connected to the city center by Metro Line E (Violet) which takes you to the Trindade station in around 25-30 minutes. Metro tickets can be purchased at the airport station. For more information on schedules and fares, visit the Metro do Porto website (https://www.metrodoporto.pt/).

2. Taxi or rideshare: Taxis and rideshare services like Uber and Bolt are available at the airport. The journey to the city center takes around 20-25 minutes, depending on traffic.

3. Airport shuttle: Several companies offer shuttle services between the airport and city center hotels. One option is Goin' Porto (https://www.goinporto.com/), which provides shared and private transfers.

4. Bus: STCP Bus 601, 602, and 3M connect the airport to various points in the city. For more information on routes and schedules, visit the STCP website (https://www.stcp.pt/).

**By Train:**

Porto has excellent train connections with other cities in Portugal and neighboring Spain. The main train stations in Porto are Campanhã and São Bento. Campanhã serves long-distance and regional trains, while São Bento mainly serves regional and suburban lines.

To search for train routes, schedules, and fares, visit the Comboios de Portugal (CP) website (https://www.cp.pt/). If you're traveling from Spain, you can check the Renfe website (http://www.renfe.com/) for international train options.

**By Bus:**

Long-distance buses connect Porto with other Portuguese cities and international destinations. The main bus terminal in Porto is Rodonorte (also known as Campo 24 de Agosto), which is a short walk or metro ride from the city center.

Some of the primary bus companies serving Porto include Rede Expressos (https://www.rede-expressos.pt/), Renex (http://www.renex.pt/), and ALSA (https://www.alsa.com/). These websites allow you to search for routes, schedules, and fares.

**By Car:**

If you prefer to drive to Porto, the city is well-connected to Portugal's extensive highway network. Major highways include the A1 (from Lisbon), A3 (from Braga and Valença), A4 (from Amarante and Bragança), and A28 (from Viana do Castelo).

To rent a car, you can use websites like Rentalcars (https://www.rentalcars.com/) or AutoEurope (https://www.autoeurope.com/) to compare prices and make reservations.

Please note that Porto's historic center features narrow streets and limited parking, so you might want to consider parking your car in a designated lot or garage outside the city center and using public transportation to explore the city.

## 2.3 Getting Around Porto

Porto is a compact and walkable city, making it easy to explore many attractions on foot. However, for longer distances or to visit specific sites, you can rely on the city's efficient public transportation system. Here's a practical guide to getting around Porto:

**1.  Metro**

The Porto Metro system comprises six color-coded lines (A, B, C, D, E, and F) connecting the city center with surrounding neighborhoods and suburbs. Key stations in the city center include Trindade, São Bento, and Bolhão. The metro is a quick and convenient way to reach attractions like Casa da Música, Estádio do Dragão, and Matosinhos beach.

Tickets can be purchased at metro stations using vending machines or ticket counters. You'll need to buy an Andante Card (€0.60), a reusable card that you can top up with credit or multi-trip passes. Single-journey tickets (Z2) cost €1.20, while a 24-hour pass (Z2) costs €4.15. Make sure to validate your ticket before boarding.

For more information on routes, schedules, and fares, visit the Metro do Porto website (https://www.metrodoporto.pt/).

**2.  Bus**

The city's bus network, operated by STCP, covers areas not serviced by the metro. Buses are an excellent option for reaching attractions like the Serralves Foundation and Foz do Douro.

Tickets can be purchased from the bus driver (€2.00 for a single journey) or using the Andante Card (€1.20 for a Z2 single journey). Note that Andante Cards must be validated on the bus.

For routes, schedules, and fare information, visit the STCP website (https://www.stcp.pt/).

**3.  Tram**

Porto's iconic trams are a charming way to explore the city. While not as extensive as the metro or bus systems, three historic tram lines (1, 18, and 22) offer scenic rides and connect some popular attractions.

Single-journey tickets can be purchased onboard for €3.00. The Andante Card is not valid on trams.

For more information on tram routes and schedules, visit the STCP website (https://www.stcp.pt/).

### 4. Funicular and Elevators

Porto's hilly terrain is served by several funiculars and elevators that provide easy access to higher points. The Funicular dos Guindais connects Ribeira with Batalha and offers stunning views of the Douro River. Tickets cost €2.50 for a single journey or can be used with a validated Andante Card.

### 5. Taxis and Rideshares

Taxis and rideshare services like Uber and Bolt are widely available in Porto. While not the most budget-friendly option, they can be convenient for late-night transportation or traveling with heavy luggage.

### 6. Bicycle

Porto's expanding network of bike lanes and bike-sharing options make it easy to explore the city on two wheels. Vodafone's GIRA bike-sharing system (https://gira-bicicletasdelisboa.pt/) offers short-term rentals, with prices starting at €2.00 for the first hour.

### 7. Porto Card

Consider purchasing a Porto Card (https://www.portocard.city) if you plan to use public transportation extensively and visit multiple attractions. The card offers unlimited use of public transport (excluding trams) and discounts or free admission to various museums and attractions. Prices start at €13.00 for a 1-day card.

### Car Rentals and Driving Tips

Porto is a beautiful city located in northern Portugal. It is known for its stunning architecture, its delicious food, and its friendly people. If you are planning a trip to Porto, there are a few things you should know about car rentals and driving tips.

When renting a car in Portugal, it is important to remember that the minimum age to rent a car is 21 years old. You will also need a valid driver's license and a credit card. It is also important to remember that Portugal drives on the right-hand side of the road.

If you are planning to rent a car in Porto, it is best to book your rental car in advance. This will allow you to get the best possible rate. When picking up your rental car, be sure to inspect the vehicle for any damage. If you find any damage, be sure to take photos and report it to the rental company.

Portugal has a few toll roads. If you are planning to use a toll road, it is important to have the correct change. Toll roads in Portugal accept cash and credit cards.

When driving in Portugal, it is important to obey the speed limit. The speed limit on highways is 120 km/h. The speed limit in urban areas is 50 km/h.

It is also important to be aware of Portugal's DUI laws. The legal blood alcohol limit in Portugal is 0.05%. If you are caught driving with a blood alcohol level above the legal limit, you will face steep fines and possibly jail time.

If you are planning a trip to Porto, a rental car can be a great option. Just be sure to remember the age requirements, driver's license requirements, and toll road information. And always obey the speed limit and Portugal's DUI laws.

# 3. Best Things to Do in Porto

If you're looking for the best things to do in Porto, you've come to the right place! This vibrant city on the Douro River is brimming with culture, history, and flavor. From its world-famous port wine and Porto Cathedral to its stunning bridges and lively nightlife, there's plenty to keep you entertained in Porto.

To help you make the most of your time in this incredible city, we've put together a list of the best things to do in Porto. So whether you're looking to sample the local wine, explore the city's historic landmarks, or just soak up the atmosphere, you'll find everything you need to know right here.

## Top 10 Things to Do in Porto

### 1. Visit the Porto Cathedral

One of the most iconic landmarks in Porto, the Porto Cathedral is a must-visit for any first-time visitor to the city. This imposing Gothic cathedral, which dates back to the 12th century, is home to a beautiful baroque interior and a stunning rose window. Make sure to climb the bell tower for sweeping views over the city.

### 2. Stroll Across the Dom Luis I Bridge

Spanning the Douro River between Porto and Vila Nova de Gaia, the Dom Luis I Bridge is one of the city's most iconic landmarks. Built in 1886, this double-deck steel bridge is a feat of engineering, and offers stunning views over the river and cityscape. If you're feeling energetic, you can even walk or cycle across the bridge.

### 3. Sample Port Wine at a Local Winery

Porto is famous for its namesake port wine, so be sure to sample some while you're in town. There are many great wineries to choose from, but our top pick is the Taylor's Winery. This historic winery offers tours, tastings, and even a restaurant, making it the perfect place to spend an afternoon.

### 4. Take a Boat Ride on the Douro River

One of the best ways to see Porto is from the water. There are many boat tour operators offering cruises up and down the Douro River, so you can sit back, relax, and take in the city's stunning bridges and riverside buildings. We recommend going at sunset for the most magical experience.

## 5. Admire the Views from Palacio da Bolsa

The Palácio da Bolsa, a 19th-century neoclassical building, once served as the city's stock exchange. Today, it is a cultural and historical attraction. Don't miss the ornate Arabian Hall and the splendid Pátio das Nações. Take a guided tour to learn more about its history and significance, and make sure to visit the terrace for panoramic views of the city.

## 6.   Wander Through the Lello Bookstore

Lello Bookstore is one of the world's most beautiful bookshops, featuring a stunning neo-Gothic interior with a red spiral staircase and stained-glass windows. It is said to have inspired J.K. Rowling during her time in Porto. Browse through the extensive collection of books and enjoy a coffee in the bookstore's small café.

## 7.   Discover Ribeira District

Ribeira is Porto's oldest district and a UNESCO World Heritage site. Wander through the narrow, winding streets lined with colorful houses, cafés, and shops. Don't miss the Praça da Ribeira, a picturesque square that offers beautiful views of the Douro River and the Dom Luis I Bridge.

## 8.   Visit the Church of São Francisco

The Church of São Francisco is a magnificent example of Gothic architecture with a jaw-dropping baroque interior. The church's opulent gilded woodwork, intricate carvings, and beautiful azulejos make it a must-visit. Don't forget to explore the church's catacombs and the museum.

## 9.   Relax at the Crystal Palace Gardens

The Crystal Palace Gardens, or Jardins do Palácio de Cristal, are a lush oasis in the heart of Porto. Stroll through the beautifully landscaped gardens, enjoy a picnic, or simply relax in the peaceful surroundings. The gardens also offer spectacular views over the Douro River and the city.

**10. Experience the Vibrant Nightlife in Galerias de Paris**

For a taste of Porto's nightlife, head to the Galerias de Paris district, a lively area filled with bars, restaurants, and clubs. Whether you're looking for a quiet drink, live music, or a night of dancing, you'll find it all in this vibrant neighborhood. The area comes alive after dark, making it the perfect place to experience Porto's energetic nightlife.

## 3.1 Top Sights to See and Visit

The city of Porto is situated on the Douro River in northwestern Portugal. As one of the oldest European centres, Porto's history goes back to the 4th century when it was an important port for trade and commerce. Today, the city is a major tourist destination known for its stunning architecture, vibrant culture and delicious food and wine. Here are some of the top sights and attractions to see and visit in Porto.

The **Ribeira District** is the historic centre of Porto and a UNESCO World Heritage Site. The district is located along the Douro River and is filled with narrow streets, medieval buildings and baroque churches. The best way to explore the Ribeira District is on foot, so take your time to wander the streets and take in the sights and sounds of this unique area.

The **Palacio da Bolsa** is one of the most impressive buildings in Porto. Built in the 19th century, the Palacio da Bolsa is a former stock exchange that now houses the Chamber of Commerce. The interior of the Palacio da Bolsa is magnificent, with opulent decoration, stained glass windows and a grand staircase. You can take a guided tour of the Palacio da Bolsa to learn more about its history and architecture.

The **São Bento Railway Station** is another Porto landmark that is worth a visit. The station was built in the early 20th century and its interior is decorated with more than 20,000 blue and white Portuguese tiles. The tiles depict scenes from Portugal's history and are a truly stunning sight.

The **Cathedral of Porto** is one of the city's most important religious landmarks. The cathedral dates back to the 12th century and is a mix of

Romanesque and Gothic styles. The exterior of the cathedral is quite plain, but the interior is beautifully decorated with carved stone and painted frescoes.

The **Lello Bookshop** is one of the most iconic places in Porto. The bookshop was founded in 1906 and is known for its stunning Art Nouveau interior. The Lello Bookshop is also said to have inspired J.K. Rowling's Harry Potter series, as she is known to have spent time in the shop while living in Porto.

No visit to Porto is complete without sampling the local food and wine. Porto is known for its delicious seafood dishes and its world-famous port wine.

## 3.2 Museums and Cultural Institutions

Porto is home to a number of museums and cultural institutions, many of which are located in the historic center of the city. The most notable of these are the Serralves Foundation, the Museu Nacional de Arte Contemporânea, the Museu do Douro, and the Casa da Música.

The **Serralves Foundation** is an art museum and cultural center that is dedicated to contemporary art and culture. The museum is home to a permanent collection of contemporary art, as well as a number of temporary exhibitions. The Serralves Foundation also hosts a variety of cultural events, including concerts, lectures, and film screenings.

The **Museu Nacional de Arte Contemporânea** is a museum that is dedicated to contemporary art from Portugal. The museum has a collection of contemporary art, as well as a number of temporary exhibitions. The Museu Nacional de Arte Contemporânea also hosts a variety of cultural events, including concerts, lectures, and film screenings.

The **Museu do Douro** is a museum that is dedicated to the history and culture of the Douro Valley. The museum has a collection of artifacts and exhibits that tell the story of the Douro Valley, from its Roman roots to its present-day incarnation. The Museu do Douro also hosts a variety of cultural events, including concerts, lectures, and film screenings.

The **Casa da Música** is a concert hall and music venue that is home to the Portuguese symphony orchestra. The Casa da Música also hosts a variety of other musical events, including concerts, opera, and ballet.

## 3.3 Parks and Outdoor Experiences

If you're looking for some outdoor fun during your stay in Porto, there are plenty of parks and outdoor experiences to enjoy. From strolling through the picturesque gardens to hiking in the lush countryside, there's something for everyone.

The most popular park in Porto is the **Parque da Cidade do Porto,** which stretches along the Douro River. This park is perfect for a leisurely stroll or a picnic lunch, and there are plenty of benches and shady spots to relax in. There are also several playgrounds for the kids, making it a great place to spend a day with the family. If you're feeling more active, you can rent a bicycle and explore the many trails that wind through the park.

Just outside of the city center, you'll find the Parque Natural da Serra do Pilar. This park is perfect for a nature hike, and there are several marked trails to follow. Be sure to bring your camera, as the views from the top of the hill are simply stunning.

For a truly unique outdoor experience, head to the **Jardim do Palacio de Cristal**. This park is home to a beautiful glass palace, which is surrounded by lush gardens. It's the perfect place to escape the hustle and bustle of the city and enjoy some peace and quiet.

If you're looking for a beach day, head to **Praia do Molhe**. This beach is located just a short drive from the city center and offers stunning views of the Atlantic Ocean. There's plenty of space to lay out a towel and relax, or you can take a dip in the refreshing waters.

No matter what your interests are, you'll be sure to find a park or outdoor experience to suit your needs in Porto.

## 3.4 Top Neighborhoods to visit

If you're planning a trip to Portugal's second city, Porto, you'll want to make sure to visit some of the best neighborhoods the city has to offer. From the picturesque streets of the Ribeira district to the lively nightlife of Boavista, there's something for everyone in Porto. Here are just a few of the city's top neighborhoods to visit on your next trip.

**The Ribeira District**

No visit to Porto would be complete without a stroll through the Ribeira district. This UNESCO World Heritage Site is located on the banks of the Rio Douro and is full of narrow, winding streets and picturesque buildings. Be sure to take a ride on the iconic Porto tram, which makes its way through the Ribeira district.

**Boavista**

If you're looking for a more modern side of Porto, head to Boavista. This chic neighborhood is home to some of the city's best shopping and dining, as well as a lively nightlife scene. Be sure to check out some of the city's most popular nightclubs, like Industria Club and Plano B.

**Foz doDouro**

For a more relaxed atmosphere, head to Foz doDouro. This seaside neighborhood is the perfect place to take a stroll, go for a swim, or just enjoy the views of the Atlantic Ocean. Foz doDouro is also home to some of Porto's best seafood restaurants, so be sure to save room for a meal by the water.

# 4. Accommodation

There are plenty of accommodation options in Porto to suit all budgets. From camping and hostels to apartments and luxury hotels, there is something for everyone.

If you're on a tight budget, there are a few hostels and camping options available. For a mid-range budget, there are plenty of apartments and hotels to choose from. For those wanting to splash out, there are a number of luxury hotels in the city.

When it comes to finding accommodation in Porto, it is best to book in advance. This is especially true during the summer months, when the city is very busy with tourists.

## 4.1 Best Areas to Stay in Porto: Pros, Cons, and Accommodation Options

There are many great areas to stay in Porto, and it really depends on what you're looking for in a vacation. If you want to be in the heart of the action and near all the best attractions, then staying in the city center is ideal. The Ribeira district is a great option, as it's right on the river and has a lot of charm. If you're looking for a more relaxed atmosphere, then staying in one of the suburbs is a better option. Foz do Douro is a popular choice, as it's right on the beach.

Here's a detailed analysis of some of the best areas to stay in Porto:

1.  **Ribeira**

Pros:

- Centrally located and within walking distance to many attractions
- Picturesque views of the Douro River and the Dom Luis I Bridge
- Numerous dining and shopping options
- Lively atmosphere

Cons:

- Can be crowded and noisy, especially during peak season

- Limited parking and narrow streets

- Accommodation options tend to be more expensive

Things to do:

- Explore the narrow, winding streets of the Ribeira district

- Visit the Palácio da Bolsa and the Church of São Francisco

- Take a Douro River cruise or stroll along the Cais da Ribeira

Top Mid-range Hotel: Carris Porto Ribeira
(https://www.carrishoteles.com/en/hotel-carris-porto-ribeira-in-porto/)
Top Luxury Hotel: Pestana Vintage Porto Hotel & World Heritage Site
(https://www.pestanacollection.com/en/hotel/pestana-vintage-porto)

## 2. Baixa (Downtown)

Pros:

- Close to many attractions, shops, and restaurants

- Excellent public transportation options

- A mix of traditional and modern architecture

- Wide range of accommodation options

Cons:

- Can be crowded and noisy, particularly during daytime

- Limited parking

Things to do:

- Visit the iconic Bolhão Market and the Majestic Café

- Explore the Clérigos Church and Tower

- Shop along Rua de Santa Catarina and Rua das Flores

Top Mid-range Hotel: Hotel Teatro (https://www.hotelteatro.pt/en/) Top
Luxury Hotel: InterContinental Porto - Palacio das Cardosas
(https://www.ihg.com/intercontinental/hotels/gb/en/porto/prtha/hoteld
etail)

### 3. Cedofeita

Pros:

- Trendy neighborhood with a bohemian atmosphere
- Numerous art galleries, boutiques, and cafés
- Quiet and less touristy than other central areas
- Easy access to public transportation

Cons:

- A bit further from some of the main attractions

Things to do:

- Visit the Centro Comercial Bombarda and its surrounding art galleries
- Stroll along Rua de Miguel Bombarda, known for its street art and design shops
- Explore the Crystal Palace Gardens

Top Mid-range Hotel: Eurostars das Artes (https://www.eurostarshotels.co.uk/eurostars-das-artes.html) Top Luxury Hotel: Rosa Et Al Townhouse (https://rosaetal.com/)

### 4. Foz do Douro

Pros:

- Beautiful coastal location with beaches and promenades
- Upscale and peaceful atmosphere
- Variety of dining options and seafront bars
- Ideal for those looking for a more relaxed stay

Cons:

- Farther from the city center and main attractions
- Limited accommodation options

Things to do:

- Relax at the beaches of Praia da Luz and Praia do Homem do Leme

- Visit the Pergola da Foz and the Fort of São Francisco do Queijo

- Stroll along the Avenida do Brasil promenade

Top Mid-range Hotel: Vila Foz Hotel & SPA (https://www.vilafozhotel.pt/en/) Top Luxury Hotel: Hotel Boa-Vista (https://www.hotelboavista.com/en)

## 4.2.1 Best Luxury Hotels

If you're looking for a luxurious hotel experience in Porto, you won't be disappointed. The city is home to a number of impressive properties, from grand 5-star hotels to more intimate boutique hotels.

In the heart of the city, the **Pestana Palacio do Freixo** is a beautiful 18th-century palace that has been converted into a luxurious hotel. The property overlooks the Douro River and offers an outdoor pool, spa, and a Michelin-starred restaurant.

For something a bit more intimate, the **Lapa Palace Hotel** is a perfect choice. This elegant property has just 27 rooms and suites, each with their own unique style. The hotel is located in a historic building in the center of Porto and features a garden and terrace with views of the city.

If you're looking for a hotel with breathtaking views, the **Yeatman Hotel** is the perfect option. This 5-star property is located on a hilltop in Vila Nova de Gaia, just across the river from Porto. The hotel has an outdoor pool, spa, and a Michelin-starred restaurant with panoramic views of the city.

If you're looking for a hotel with a bit more history, **the Hotel Infante de Sagres** is a great choice. This 5-star hotel is located in a 19th-century building in the center of Porto. The hotel features an outdoor pool, spa, and a Michelin-starred restaurant.

### 4.2.2 Best Mid-Range Hotels

If you're looking for a comfortable place to stay in Porto without breaking the bank, there are plenty of great mid-range hotels to choose from. Here are some of our top picks:

Hotel da Música: This modern hotel is located in the heart of Porto's music district, just a short walk from the city's main concert hall. The rooms are spacious and bright, and the staff are incredibly friendly and helpful.

Hotel Teatro: This hotel is located in a renovated 19th-century theatre, and retains many original features such as the grand staircase and chandeliers. The rooms are elegant and comfortable, and the breakfast buffet is one of the best in the city.

Hotel do Norte: This hotel is located in a beautiful Art Deco building in the centre of Porto. The rooms are spacious and decorated in a traditional style, and the views from the roof terrace are stunning.

Hotel Mercure Porto Centro: This modern hotel is located in the centre of Porto, just a short walk from the main shopping street. The rooms are comfortable and well-equipped, and the staff are very friendly and helpful.

### 4.2.3 Best Budget Hotels

In Porto, there are many different types of hotels to choose from, depending on your budget. For those looking for the best budget hotels in the city, there are a few options that stand out above the rest.

The first option for budget hotels in Porto is the Hotel da Música. This hotel is located in the heart of the city, and offers guests a great location for exploring all that Porto has to offer. The rooms at the Hotel da Música are clean and comfortable, and the staff is friendly and helpful.

Another great option for budget hotels in Porto is the Hotel do Norte. This hotel is located in the city center, and offers guests a great location for exploring all that Porto has to offer. The rooms at the Hotel do Norte are clean and comfortable, and the staff is friendly and helpful.

A third option for budget hotels in Porto is the Hotel Dom Henrique. This hotel is located in the city center, and offers guests a great location for exploring all that Porto has to offer. The rooms at the Hotel Dom Henrique are clean and comfortable, and the staff is friendly and helpful.

# 5. Food and Drink

Porto is a city with a strong food culture, and there are plenty of options for eating and drinking here. The city is home to a number of Michelin-starred restaurants, as well as more casual eateries serving up local specialties.

There are also many bars and clubs in Porto, which make for great nightlife options. Whether you're looking for a place to have a few drinks or dance the night away, you'll find plenty of options in Porto.

If you're looking to try some of the local food, there are a few dishes that you shouldn't miss. One of the most popular is **francesinha,** a sandwich that is typically made with meat, cheese, and a tomato and beer sauce.

Other popular dishes include **caldo verde** (a soup made with potatoes, kale, and sausage), **bacalhau** (dried and salted cod), **and tripas a moda do Porto** (tripe in a Porto-style stew).

Porto is renowned for its rich wine culture, with numerous wineries and wine bars offering a wide range of varieties for you to savor. Some popular wine bars include Capela Incomum, Wine Quay Bar, and Vinologia.

However, if wine isn't your preference, the city also boasts a thriving beer scene. Local breweries are gaining traction, and you can find a selection of craft beers at various bars and pubs throughout Porto. Some notable breweries and beer-centric establishments include Catraio Craft Beer Shop, Cervejaria do Carmo, and Letraria Craft Beer Garden.

For coffee enthusiasts, Porto does not disappoint. The city is dotted with charming cafes that serve excellent coffee and a variety of specialty drinks, such as cappuccinos and lattes. Be sure to visit some of the city's best cafes, like Majestic Café, Moustache Coffee House, and Almada 13, where you can enjoy a perfect cup of coffee and a delightful ambiance.

## 5.1 Porto's Culinary Scene

In a city as old as Porto, it's no surprise that its culinary scene has been shaped by a rich history and diverse influences. The city's chefs take advantage of the freshest local ingredients to create traditional Portuguese dishes with a modern twist.

Porto is known for its seafood, and you'll find no shortage of restaurants serving up fresh catches of the day. If you're looking for something a bit more hearty, try the traditional Portuguese dish of **cozido à portuguesa**, a stew made with various meats, vegetables, and spices.

For a sweet treat, be sure to try a **pastel de nata,** a traditional Portuguese custard tart. These tarts are widely available throughout the city, but they're especially delicious at the Pasteis de Belém, a bakery that's been serving them since 1837.

If you're looking to sample some of the best wines the city has to offer, head to one of Porto's many wine bars. Many of these bars offer small plates of food to accompany your wine, making them the perfect spot for a light meal or snack.

## 5.2 Local Traditional Dishes and Specialties

In Portugal's second city, Porto, there are plenty of local dishes and specialties to try. Here are five of the most popular:

1. Francesinha: This hearty dish is a sandwich made with bread, ham, sausage, and steak, and covered in melted cheese and a hot sauce. It's often served with a side of fries.

2. Tripas à Moda do Porto: This traditional dish is made with white beans, pork, and cabbage.

3. Bacalhau à Gomes de Sá: This is a cod dish that is popular in Portugal. It is made with potatoes, onions, and garlic.

4. Arroz de Pato: This dish is made with duck, rice, and vegetables.

5. Pasteis de Nata: These are Portugal's famous egg custard tarts and they originated in Lisbon. However, you can find them all over Portugal, including in Porto.

Below you can find our suggested local Portuguese dishes that you should try in order to enhance your culinary experience, while you are at Porto.

In Portugal, codfish is used in innumerous dishes, and it is seen as the country's food symbol. However, Portuguese gastronomy is much more than just the "Bacalhau." Portugal's cuisine is very rich and diverse, and there are many typical and incomparable meals you most definitely have to try while you are here.

Below, there will be a few examples of local dishes that you should taste to enhance your culinary experience, while you are in Porto.

1. **Pastel De Nata [Portuguese]: Custard Pie**

The Pastel de Belém was elected, in 2011, as one of the 7 Wonders of Gastronomy of Portugal. As mentioned above, the original recipe is still a secret very well kept by the first pastry shop that sold these. Situated in Belém, Pastéis de Belém offers the most original and traditional pastel de nata there is. They are served hot out of the baking oven, with cinnamon and powdered sugar on top. Only the ones that come from this shop may be called Pastéis de Belém. All the others are merely pastéis de nata. In spite of this, currently, there is an increasing number of pastry shops recreating this unique delicacy, and successfully. Now, you can find it in any coffee shop throughout Portugal, and even abroad. Some of them even compete with the original for the tastiest pastel de nata there is.

**2. Travesseiro de Sintra [Portuguese]: Sintra's Pillow**

One of the main delicacies Sintra is known for. Every year, millions of tourists, and Portuguese, visit the famous "Piriquita" to try one of these, but there are currently shops in the Porto center that sell this pastry.

3. Queijadas [Portuguese]:

Queijada is another pastry famously made in Sintra. It has many variations currently, but originaly its recipe consists of cheese, eggs, milk, and sugar.

**4. Cozido à Portuguesa [Portuguese]: Portuguese Stew**

Cozido à Portuguesa, or Portuguese Stew, is a traditional and hearty dish that showcases the rich flavors and culinary diversity of Portugal. This beloved meal is composed of a variety of meats, such as beef, pork, and chicken, alongside regional sausages like chouriço and morcela, all slow-cooked to tender perfection. The dish also features an assortment of vegetables, including potatoes, carrots, turnips, and cabbage, which absorb the delicious flavors of the meats and sausages as they cook. Each region of Portugal adds its unique touch to the recipe, often incorporating local ingredients and cooking methods. Cozido à Portuguesa is typically enjoyed as a family meal, bringing people together to savor the warmth and comfort of this quintessential Portuguese dish.

### 7. Caldo Verde [Portuguese]: Green Broth

A very popular soup in Portugal with chorizo and potatoes, collard greens, olive oil and salt!

8. Arroz-doce [Portuguese]: Rice Pudding

A sweet dessert made of rice, milk, eggs and lemon zest.

## 9. Bacalhau à Zé do Pipo [Pt]: Cod, in Ze do Pipo Style

Bacalhau à Zé do Pipo, or Cod in Ze do Pipo Style, is a classic Portuguese dish that celebrates the country's love affair with bacalhau, or salted cod. This flavorful recipe is named after a famous tavern owner from Porto, Zé do Pipo, who was known for his delectable cod creations. The dish features tender flakes of salted cod that are cooked and then mixed with sautéed onions and garlic. The cod mixture is then topped with a layer of smooth and creamy mashed potatoes, which are often piped into elegant patterns for an attractive presentation. The dish is finished with a garnish of black olives and a sprinkling of paprika before being baked in the oven until golden and bubbly. Bacalhau à Zé do Pipo is a rich and comforting meal that showcases the versatility and enduring popularity of salted cod in Portuguese cuisine.

## 10. Queijo Serra da Estrela [Pt]: Serra Da Estrela Cheese

Queijo Serra da Estrela, or Serra da Estrela Cheese, is a prized artisanal cheese originating from the Serra da Estrela region in central Portugal.

33

This delectable cheese is made from the raw milk of Bordaleira sheep, a breed native to the area, and boasts a unique combination of flavors and textures. With a slightly crumbly yet creamy consistency, Queijo Serra da Estrela is known for its distinctive, tangy taste that comes from the use of cardoon thistle as a coagulant, rather than traditional rennet. The cheese is typically aged for a minimum of 30 days, although some variations can be aged for up to several months, resulting in a stronger flavor and firmer texture. Often enjoyed on its own or with a slice of fresh bread, Queijo Serra da Estrela is a delicious and authentic representation of Portugal's rich cheese-making tradition.

### 11. **Ovos Moles de Aveiro** [Pt], Soft Eggs from Aveiro [En]

These soft eggs are a local delicacy from Aveiro and are made only of egg yolks and sugar. After that, the mixture is put inside of a small rice paper casing in nautical shapes, such as shells or fish

### 12. **Peixinhos da Horta [Pt], Peixinhos da Horta (Tempura) [En]**

Peixinhos da Horta, or Tempura Green Beans, is a delightful Portuguese appetizer that showcases the country's culinary ingenuity and fusion of flavors. The name "Peixinhos da Horta" translates to "little fish from the

garden," a playful reference to the appearance of the green beans, which resemble small, colorful fish when coated in the crispy batter. This traditional dish is believed to have inspired the Japanese tempura technique, introduced by Portuguese missionaries and traders in the 16th century. To prepare Peixinhos da Horta, fresh green beans are dipped in a light and airy batter made from flour, water, and sometimes egg, before being deep-fried to golden perfection. The resulting dish is a delicious combination of tender, flavorful green beans encased in a crisp, delicate coating. Peixinhos da Horta is a popular appetizer or side dish in Portugal, enjoyed with a squeeze of lemon and often accompanied by a flavorful dipping sauce.

### 13. Caldeirada de Peixe [Pt], Portuguese Fish Stew [En]

Caldeirada de Peixe, or Portuguese Fish Stew, is a mouthwatering dish that pays homage to Portugal's abundant seafood offerings and coastal heritage. This aromatic and comforting stew features a medley of fish and shellfish, such as white fish, monkfish, shrimp, and clams, combined with a rich, flavorful broth made from tomatoes, onions, garlic, bell peppers, and white wine. Herbs like parsley, cilantro, and bay leaves are added to enhance the depth of flavors, while potatoes are included to provide heartiness and substance. The dish is typically slow-cooked to allow the various ingredients to meld together, creating a harmonious and satisfying meal. Caldeirada de Peixe is often enjoyed with a side of crusty bread, perfect for sopping up the delicious, savory broth. This traditional Portuguese dish showcases the country's love of seafood and its ability to transform simple, fresh ingredients into a delectable and soul-warming culinary experience.

### 14. Tosta Mista [Portuguese]:

A tosta mista is a ham and cheese sandwich pressed together, making the cheese melt, and with a lot of salted butter on it.

## 15. Bifana [Portuguese]:

Bifana, a simple yet beloved Portuguese sandwich, is a testament to the country's ability to create culinary magic with just a few humble ingredients. This iconic street food features a tender, thinly-sliced pork cutlet marinated in a flavorful blend of garlic, white wine, paprika, and sometimes piri-piri sauce for an added kick. The marinated pork is then quickly pan-fried, allowing it to absorb the aromatic flavors while remaining juicy and succulent. The cooked pork is nestled between two slices of crusty bread, often a soft, slightly toasted Portuguese roll known as a "papo-seco." The sandwich is sometimes garnished with mustard, mayonnaise, or a simple tomato and lettuce combo, but the star of the show is undoubtedly the savory, seasoned pork. Bifanas can be found at street food vendors, cafes, and snack bars across Portugal, providing a delicious and satisfying meal that is perfect for enjoying on-the-go or as a quick, comforting snack.

## 5.3 Vegetarian and Vegan Options

Porto is a haven for vegetarians and vegans, with a wide range of options available throughout the city. Whether you're looking for a quick bite or a sit-down meal, you'll be able to find something to suit your needs.

One of the best places to start your search is at the Mercado do Bolhão, where you'll find a number of stalls selling fresh fruits and vegetables. There's also a great selection of takeaway options, such as salads and veggie wraps.

For something a little heartier, why not head to one of Porto's many vegetarian and vegan restaurants? Amongst the most popular are Botequim Bottega and Restaurante L'Artisane. Both offer a wide range of dishes, all of which are clearly labelled as vegetarian or vegan.

If you're looking for something sweet, you'll be spoilt for choice in Porto. The city is home to a number of vegan-friendly bakeries, such as Padaria Rosa and Bolos da Lili, where you can indulge in a variety of cakes, pastries and other sweet treats.

## 5.4 Savor the Flavors of Porto: Five Delightful Combo Meals

Indulge in Porto's rich culinary scene by trying out these five delightful combo meals, each featuring a carefully curated selection of appetizers, main courses, desserts, and drinks. These combinations showcase the city's unique flavors and traditional Portuguese dishes, ensuring a memorable dining experience in Porto.

**Combo Meal 1: "The Classic Porto Experience"**

- Appetizer: Bolinhos de Bacalhau (codfish cakes)

- Main Course: Francesinha (a Porto specialty sandwich with layers of meat, cheese, and a rich tomato-beer sauce)

- Dessert: Pastel de Nata (traditional Portuguese egg custard tart)

- Drink: Vinho Verde (a young, slightly sparkling Portuguese wine)

**Combo Meal 2: "A Taste of the Sea"**

- Appetizer: Caldo Verde (a hearty green soup with potatoes, kale, and chorizo)

- Main Course: Arroz de Marisco (a flavorful seafood rice dish with shrimp, clams, and mussels)

- Dessert: Leite-Creme (a Portuguese-style crème brûlée)

- Drink: White Port and Tonic (a refreshing cocktail made with white Port wine and tonic water)

**Combo Meal 3: "The Meat Lover's Delight"**

- Appetizer: Sardinha Assada (grilled sardines)

- Main Course: Posta à Mirandesa (a tender, juicy steak served with potatoes and vegetables)

- Dessert: Bolo de Bolacha (a Portuguese biscuit cake)

- Drink: Douro Valley Red Wine (a robust red wine from the nearby Douro Valley region)

**Combo Meal 4: "The Veggie Indulgence"**

- Appetizer: Salada de Polvo (octopus salad)

- Main Course: Alheira de Mirandela (a flavorful smoked sausage dish made with bread and vegetables, served with fries and rice)

- Dessert: Pudim Abade de Priscos (a silky, caramelized bacon pudding)

- Drink: Super Bock or Sagres (popular Portuguese lagers)

**Combo Meal 5: "A Fusion of Flavors"**

- Appetizer: Ameijoas à Bulhão Pato (clams cooked in a white wine, garlic, and cilantro sauce)

- Main Course: Bacalhau à Brás (a comforting codfish dish with potatoes, onions, and eggs)

- Dessert: Toucinho do Céu (a rich almond and egg yolk cake)

- Drink: Port Wine (a glass of Porto's famous fortified wine)

## 5.5 Wine and Cocktail Bars

If you're looking for a place to enjoy a glass of wine or a cocktail while in Porto, you won't be disappointed. The city is home to a number of wine and cocktail bars that are sure to please. Here are five of the best:

1. Vinho Verde Wine Bar: This wine bar is the perfect place to enjoy a glass of Vinho Verde, a type of wine that is unique to Portugal. The bar also offers a variety of other Portuguese wines, as well as a selection of tapas.

2. Bodega Ribeira: Bodega Ribeira is a popular wine bar located in the Ribeira district. The bar offers a wide selection of wines, as well as a menu of small plates.

3. wine & soul: wine & soul is a modern wine bar with an extensive list of international wines. The bar also serves a selection of small plates.

4. Tasca do Chico: Tasca do Chico is a traditional Portuguese tavern that offers a wide selection of wines and cocktails. The tavern also serves a variety of traditional Portuguese dishes.

5. Bar Velha: Bar Velha is a classic Portuguese bar that offers a wide selection of wines, cocktails, and beers. The bar also has a menu of small plates.


## 5.6 Traditional Markets

Looking for a truly authentic Porto experience? Then head to one of the city's traditional markets - where you'll find an incredible array of fresh produce, seafood, and more.

**Mercado do Bolhão** is perhaps the most well-known market in Porto, and has been in operation since 1842. Located in the city centre, it's the perfect place to stock up on fresh fruit and vegetables, as well as delicious seafood. If you're feeling hungry, there are also a number of stalls selling traditional Portuguese dishes.

Just a short walk from Mercado do Bolhão is another of Porto's markets, **Mercado de São Bento.** This market is smaller than Mercado do Bolhão, but is no less atmospheric. It's particularly well-known for its stunning tilework, which depicts scenes from Portuguese history. As well as fresh produce, you'll also find a range of stalls selling flowers, books, and other knick-knacks.

If you're looking for something a little different, head **to Mercado de Ribeira**. This market is located on the banks of the River Douro, and is the perfect place to buy fresh seafood. There are also a number of cafes and restaurants, making it the perfect spot to take a break and enjoy a meal with a view.

No matter which market you choose to visit, you're sure to have a memorable experience. So head to one of Porto's traditional markets and discover the city's hidden treasures.

## 5.7 Top Things to Do for Foodies in Porto

1. Explore Mercado do Bolhão – Immerse yourself in the vibrant atmosphere of Porto's central market, where you can find fresh produce, seafood, and traditional Portuguese delicacies. Experience the local culture and shop for ingredients to cook a delicious meal.

2. Savor the iconic Francesinha – Don't miss trying Porto's famous Francesinha at Café Santiago (http://www.cafesantiago.pt) or Bufete Fase (https://www.facebook.com/BufeteFase/). This hearty sandwich is filled with meat, cheese, and ham, and smothered in a rich tomato and beer sauce.

3. Join a foodie walking tour – Taste Porto (https://www.tasteporto.com/) and Porto Food Tours (https://portofoodtours.com/) offer guided culinary tours led by local experts. Discover Porto's hidden gems, sample traditional dishes, and learn about the city's rich food culture.

4. Experience a local winery – Visit the Douro Valley, one of Portugal's most renowned wine regions. Many wineries, such as Quinta do Vallado (https://www.quintadovallado.com) and Quinta do Crasto (https://www.quintadocrasto.pt), offer tours and tastings, allowing you to sample their finest wines.

5. Indulge in traditional Portuguese pastries – Treat yourself to the famous Portuguese custard tart, pastel de nata, at Manteigaria

(https://www.facebook.com/manteigariaporto/) or Nata Lisboa (https://www.natalisboa.com/). Be sure to sample other delicious pastries as you explore Porto's culinary scene.

6.  Dine by the riverside – The Ribeira district boasts a lively atmosphere and numerous restaurants with stunning river views. Enjoy a meal at D.Tonho (http://www.dtonho.com/) or Jimão Tapas e Vinhos (https://jimaotapasvinhos.com/) for a memorable dining experience.

7.  Participate in a cooking class – Learn how to prepare Porto's signature dishes at a hands-on cooking class led by a professional chef. Cook in Ribeira (https://www.cookinribeira.com/) and Porto Cooking Academy (https://portocookingacademy.pt/) offer classes that will enrich your culinary skills and knowledge.

## 5.8 Best Local Restaurants (Luxury, Mid Range and Budget Suggestions)

**Luxury**

1. Gusto Wine & Dine - This restaurant is perfect for those who want to enjoy a luxurious dining experience while in Porto. The menu features a wide variety of both local and international dishes, and the wine list is impressive. The setting is elegant and the service is excellent.

2. The Yeatman - The Yeatman is a Michelin-starred restaurant that offers an unforgettable dining experience. The menu features creative takes on traditional Portuguese dishes, and the wine list is one of the best in the city. The setting is stunning, with views of the Douro River, and the service is impeccable.

3. Fifty Seconds - Fifty Seconds is a rooftop restaurant with breathtaking views of the city. The menu features both local and international dishes, and the wine list is impressive. The setting is chic and modern, and the service is attentive.

**Mid-Range**

1. Mercado Bom Sucesso - Mercado Bom Sucesso is a great option for those looking for a mid-range dining option. The restaurant is located in a market, and the menu features a variety of fresh, local dishes. The setting is casual and the service is friendly.

2. Taberna do Largo - Taberna do Largo is a cozy restaurant that offers a taste of traditional Portuguese cuisine. The menu features a variety of dishes made with fresh, local ingredients, and the setting is rustic and charming. The service is attentive and the prices are reasonable.

3. Tasca da Esquina - Tasca da Esquina is a great option for those looking for a mid-range dining option. The menu features a variety of traditional Portuguese dishes, and the setting is cozy and charming. The service is friendly and the prices are reasonable.

**Budget**

1. Cafeteria Guarany - Cafeteria Guarany is a great option for those on a budget. The menu features a variety of simple, yet tasty, dishes, and the prices are very reasonable. The setting is casual and the service is friendly.

2. Restaurante do Bairro - Restaurante do Bairro is a great option for those on a budget. The menu features a variety of traditional Portuguese dishes, and the prices are reasonable. The setting is casual and the service is friendly.

# 6. Shopping

## 6.1 Fashion and Design Boutiques

In the city of Porto, fashion and design boutiques are aplenty. From high-end designer labels to more affordable and trendy stores, there is something to suit every taste and budget. Here are just a few of the many fashion and design boutiques that can be found in Porto:

Labels: This designer fashion boutique is located in the heart of the city and offers a wide range of high-end labels, such as Gucci, Prada, and Dolce & Gabbana.

Dolce Vita: Another designer fashion store, Dolce Vita stocks a wide range of luxury brands, such as Valentino, Givenchy, and Fendi.

Pois: This is a more affordable fashion store that offers a trendy and stylish selection of clothing and accessories.

Salsa: This store specializes in Latin-inspired fashion and has a wide range of colorful and fun clothes and accessories.

Tricot: This store is perfect for those who love knitwear, as it offers a wide range of sweaters, cardigans, and other knitted items.

So, whatever your fashion or design needs, you are sure to find a boutique to suit you in the city of Porto.

## 6.2 Local Art and Craft Shops

If you're looking for a unique souvenir or a one-of-a-kind gift, Porto's local art and craft shops are the perfect places to find it. Scattered throughout the city, these shops offer a wide variety of items, from traditional Portuguese pottery to handmade jewelry and everything in between.

Some of the most popular shops include A Vida Portuguesa, which specializes in traditional Portuguese products, and Loja das Meias, which sells a wide variety of colorful socks and other knitwear. For something truly unique, check out Estufa Fria, an old-fashioned greenhouse turned art gallery that sells everything from paintings to sculptures.

## 6.3 Popular Shopping Centers

Porto is home to a variety of popular shopping centers that offer an array of merchandise and services. From high-end retail stores to discount outlets, there is something for everyone in Porto.

The Clerigos Tower is one of the most popular shopping centers in Porto. The tower is home to a variety of retail stores, as well as a food court and a cinema. The Clerigos Tower is a great place to find gifts for friends and family, as well as a wide variety of items for your own personal use.

The Porto Shopping Center is another popular shopping destination in Porto. The center is home to over 200 stores, as well as a food court, a cinema, and a bowling alley. The Porto Shopping Center is the perfect place to spend a day if you're looking for a wide variety of things to do.

The Metro Center is a popular shopping center in Porto that is home to a variety of retail stores, as well as a food court and a cinema. The Metro Center is a great place to find gifts for friends and family, as well as a wide variety of items for your own personal use.

The Porto Airport is home to a variety of retail stores, as well as a food court and a cinema. The Porto Airport is a great place to find gifts for friends and family, as well as a wide variety of items for your own personal use.

The Vasco da Gama Shopping Center is a popular shopping center in Porto that is home to a variety of retail stores, as well as a food court and a cinema. The Vasco da Gama Shopping Center is a great place to find gifts for friends and family, as well as a wide variety of items for your own personal use.

## 6.4 Souvenirs and Gifts

Porto is a charming city with a unique atmosphere, and it is no surprise that many visitors want to take a piece of it home with them in the form of a souvenir or gift. There are plenty of options available, from the traditional to the quirky, and there is sure to be something to suit every taste and budget.

The most popular souvenirs from Porto are undoubtedly the traditional **azulejo tiles**. These beautiful blue and white ceramic tiles are used to decorate many of the city's buildings, and can be found in a variety of designs. They make for lovely gifts and souvenirs, and can be bought in tile shops and some department stores.

Another popular option is Port wine. This rich, sweet wine is produced in the surrounding region and makes for a lovely gift or after-dinner treat. It is available in a range of prices and styles, so it is easy to find something to suit your budget.

For those looking for something a little more unusual, there are a number of quirky Porto-themed gifts available. These include items such as keyrings and magnets featuring the city's famous bridges, ornaments shaped like the traditional tramcars, and even bottles of port wine with custom-designed labels.

# 7. Nightlife and Entertainment

There is no shortage of things to do in Porto after dark. The city's nightlife scene is vibrant and diverse, with something to suit all tastes.

For those who want to enjoy a few drinks in a relaxed setting, there are plenty of bars and pubs to choose from. The historic centre is particularly well-stocked with atmospheric watering holes, many of which are located in atmospheric converted warehouses.

If you're looking for something a little livelier, there are also a number of clubs and music venues to check out. These range from small, intimate clubs playing underground music, to huge superclubs that stay open until the early hours.

Whatever your taste, you're sure to find somewhere to suit you in Porto's nightlife scene.

## 7.1 Bars and Clubs

In Porto, there are many different types of bars and clubs to suit every taste. For those who want to enjoy a quiet drink in a relaxed atmosphere, there are plenty of traditional bars serving local wines and delicacies. For those who are looking for a more lively evening out, there are clubs playing everything from techno to traditional Portuguese music. And for those who just want to have a good time, there are plenty of bars and clubs to choose from.

To help you decide where to go, here is a list of some of the best bars and clubs in Porto:

Casa da Musica: This is one of the most popular clubs in Porto and it is easy to see why. Located in a converted warehouse, it has a huge dance floor and a great sound system. There is also a restaurant and a terrace for those who want to take a break from dancing.

Capela Inclinada: This club is located in an old chapel and it has a very unique atmosphere. It is small and intimate with a great sound system.

Botequim Bottega: This is a great place for those who want to try some of the local wines. It has a relaxed atmosphere and there is often live music.

Bourbon Street: This club is located in an old church and it has a very unique atmosphere. It is small and intimate with a great sound system.

 Industria: This club is located in an old factory and it has a very unique atmosphere. It is large and spacious with a great sound system.

These are just some of the bars and clubs that you will find in Porto. If you are looking for a specific type of music or atmosphere, you are sure to find a place that suits your taste.

## 7.2 Live Music and Cultural Performances

Porto is home to a vibrant music and culture scene, with live music and cultural performances happening throughout the city. From classical concerts and operas at the Palacio da Bolsa to folk music and traditional dances at the Casa da Música, there is something for everyone to enjoy.

The Palacio da Bolsa is one of the most iconic buildings in Porto and hosts a variety of classical concerts and operas throughout the year. The Palacio da Música is another popular venue for live music, with a programme that includes everything from traditional Portuguese folk music to contemporary jazz.

For those looking to experience some traditional Portuguese culture, the Casa da Música is the perfect place to go. Here, you can watch folk dances, listen to traditional music, and even learn how to make some of Portugal's iconic dishes.

If you're looking for a more unique cultural experience, be sure to check out the Porto Street Art Festival. This annual event transforms the streets of Porto into a giant outdoor gallery, with local and international artists displaying their work for all to see.

## 7.3 Festivals and Events

There are many festivals and events that take place in Porto throughout the year. The most popular ones are the following:

- **Sao Joao Festival:** This festival is held every year on the night of the 23rd of June and is one of the most popular and well-attended festivals in the city. It is a celebration of St. John the Baptist, the patron saint of Porto, and features a lot of traditional music and dancing.

- **Porto Wine Festival:** This festival is held in early September and is one of the biggest events in the city. It celebrates the city's world-famous wine industry and features wine tastings, food stalls, and live music.

- **New Year's Eve:** Porto's New Year's Eve celebrations are some of the best in the country, with a huge street party taking place in the city centre.

## 7.4 Family-Friendly Entertainment

If you're looking for family-friendly entertainment in Porto, you won't have to look far. The city has plenty to offer in terms of activities and attractions that will appeal to both kids and adults.

One of the most popular family-friendly attractions in Porto is the Serralves Foundation. This world-renowned museum is home to a variety of permanent and temporary exhibitions, as well as a spacious park that's perfect for a picnic or a leisurely stroll.

If your kids are looking for a little more excitement, they'll love the Funicular dos Guindais. This historic cable car takes passengers on a short but scenic ride up to the top of one of Porto's hills, offering stunning views of the city.

For something a little more hands-on, head to the Portuguese Aquarium. Located in the heart of the city, this aquarium is home to a diverse range of marine life, including sharks, rays, and turtles. Kids will love getting up close to the underwater creatures, and there are also plenty of interactive exhibits to keep them entertained.

No visit to Porto would be complete without taking a ride on the iconic Vintage Tram. These historic streetcars offer a unique way to see the city, and kids will love riding through the streets on one of these old-fashioned vehicles.

Finally, no trip to Porto would be complete without indulging in some of the city's famous food. Porto is known for its fresh seafood, and there are plenty of restaurants that offer kid-friendly options. For a truly unique dining experience, head to the Mercado do Bolhão, where you can find a variety of food stalls selling everything from fresh fruits and vegetables to grilled meats and seafood.

# 8. Best Day Trips from Porto

There are many great day trips that can be taken from Porto. Here are eight of the best:

## 1. Guimarães

Guimarães is a city located in northwestern Portugal. It is known as the birthplace of Portugal, as it is here that the country's first king, Afonso Henriques, was born in the 12th century. The city is home to a number of historic landmarks, including the Castle of Guimarães, which was declared a UNESCO World Heritage Site in 2001. Guimarães is also home to a number of museums, including the Museum of Alberto Sampaio, which is dedicated to the city's history.

**Day Trip Itinerary to Guimarães from Porto**

08:00 – Depart from Porto Start your day at São Bento Railway Station in Porto. Catch the train to Guimarães, which usually takes around 1 hour and 15 minutes. Trains run frequently throughout the day, and you can check the schedule and ticket prices on the Comboios de Portugal website (https://www.cp.pt/).

09:15 – Arrive in Guimarães Upon arrival in Guimarães, take a few minutes to get your bearings and enjoy a quick coffee at a local café near the train station.

09:30 – Visit the Castle of Guimarães Start your exploration at the Castle of Guimarães, the city's most iconic landmark and the birthplace of the first king of Portugal. Wander around the castle grounds and take in the stunning views of the surrounding area.

10:30 – Discover the Palace of the Dukes of Braganza Next, visit the nearby Palace of the Dukes of Braganza, a 15th-century palace with an impressive collection of art, furniture, and tapestries. Learn about the history of the Braganza family and admire the palace's unique architecture.

11:30 – Explore the Historic Center Head to the historic center of Guimarães, a UNESCO World Heritage Site. Stroll through the charming streets, admire the well-preserved medieval buildings, and visit the Church of São Miguel do Castelo.

12:30 – Lunch Break Enjoy a leisurely lunch at a local restaurant, such as Histórico by Papaboa (http://www.historicobypapaboa.com/) or Restaurante São Gião (https://www.facebook.com/restaurantesaogiao/), where you can savor traditional Portuguese cuisine.

14:00 – Visit the Museu de Alberto Sampaio After lunch, visit the Museu de Alberto Sampaio, a museum dedicated to the city's history, art, and religious artifacts. Marvel at the rich collection and gain a deeper understanding of Guimarães' cultural heritage.

15:00 – Relax at Largo da Oliveira and Largo do Toural Take a break at Largo da Oliveira, a picturesque square lined with historic buildings and outdoor cafés. Then, walk to Largo do Toural, another charming square, and enjoy some shopping or people-watching.

16:30 – Take the Cable Car to Penha Mountain Ride the cable car (Teleférico de Guimarães) up to Penha Mountain, which offers panoramic views of Guimarães and the surrounding area. Spend some time exploring the nature trails and admiring the scenery.

18:00 – Return to Guimarães City Center Take the cable car back down to the city center and spend some time exploring any areas you may have missed earlier.

19:00 – Dinner in Guimarães Before heading back to Porto, enjoy a delicious dinner at a local restaurant, such as A Cozinha por António Loureiro (https://www.acozinharestaurante.com/) or Taberna Londrina (https://www.facebook.com/tabernalondrina/).

20:30 – Depart from Guimarães Return to the Guimarães train station and catch a train back to Porto. Check the train schedule on the Comboios de Portugal website (https://www.cp.pt/).

21:45 – Arrive in Porto Arrive back in Porto, bringing your day trip to Guimarães to a close.

Note: The best time to visit Guimarães is between April and October when the weather is pleasant and mild. However, the city can also be enjoyed during the off-peak months, as long as you're prepared for cooler temperatures and occasional rain. Guimarães is a charming and historic city that offers a rich cultural experience, no matter when you choose to visit.

## 2. Viana do Castelo

Viana do Castelo is a city located in northern Portugal. It is known for its beautiful beaches, its historic center, and its many festivals and events. The city is home to a number of landmarks, including the Church of Santa Luzia, which was built in the 14th century, and the Fortress of São João Baptista, which was built in the 16th century. Viana do Castelo is also home to a number of museums, including the Museum of Contemporary Art, which houses a collection of contemporary art from Portugal and around the world.

Day Trip Itinerary to Viana do Castelo from Porto

08:00 – Depart from Porto Start your day at Campanhã Railway Station in Porto. Catch the train to Viana do Castelo, which usually takes around 1 hour and 20 minutes. Trains run frequently throughout the day, and you can check the schedule and ticket prices on the Comboios de Portugal website (https://www.cp.pt/).

09:20 – Arrive in Viana do Castelo Upon arrival in Viana do Castelo, take a few minutes to get your bearings and enjoy a quick coffee at a local café near the train station.

09:45 – Explore the Historic Center Begin your exploration in the historic center of Viana do Castelo. Wander through the narrow streets, admiring the colorful buildings adorned with intricate azulejos. Make sure to stop by the Praça da República, the city's main square, and visit the beautiful 16th-century Misericórdia Church.

11:00 – Visit the Santa Luzia Sanctuary Take a taxi or the funicular up to the Santa Luzia Sanctuary, a beautiful basilica located on a hill overlooking the city. The sanctuary's stunning architecture and panoramic views of the city, the Lima River, and the Atlantic Ocean are not to be missed.

12:00 – Lunch Break Head back down to the city center and enjoy a leisurely lunch at a local restaurant, such as O Pescador (https://www.opescador.pt/) or Tasquinha da Linda (http://www.tasquinha-da-linda.com/), where you can savor fresh seafood and traditional Portuguese cuisine.

14:00 – Visit the Gil Eannes Ship Museum After lunch, head to the Gil Eannes Ship Museum, a former hospital ship that has been transformed into a fascinating museum. Learn about the history of the ship and its role in the Portuguese cod fishing industry, and explore the restored medical facilities, crew quarters, and engine room.

15:00 – Stroll Along the Riverfront Spend some time strolling along the Lima River waterfront, taking in the views and the atmosphere. If you're interested in shopping, visit the nearby streets, which are lined with local boutiques and artisan shops.

16:00 – Visit the Museu do Traje (Costume Museum) Discover the history of traditional Portuguese clothing at the Museu do Traje, which showcases an extensive collection of regional costumes and textiles, as well as jewelry and other accessories.

17:00 – Relax at the Praia do Cabedelo Head to the Praia do Cabedelo, a beautiful beach located just across the river from Viana do Castelo. Enjoy some time relaxing on the sand or taking a refreshing dip in the ocean.

18:30 – Dinner in Viana do Castelo Before heading back to Porto, enjoy a delicious dinner at a local restaurant, such as Água na Boca (https://www.facebook.com/AguaNaBoca.viana/) or Casa de Pasto Maria de Perre (https://www.facebook.com/CasaDePastoMariaDePerre/).

20:00 – Depart from Viana do Castelo Return to the Viana do Castelo train station and catch a train back to Porto. Check the train schedule on the Comboios de Portugal website (https://www.cp.pt/).

21:20 – Arrive in Porto Arrive back in Porto, bringing your day trip to Viana do Castelo to a close.

Note: The best time to visit Viana do Castelo is between April and October when the weather is pleasant and mild. However, the city can be enjoyed during the off-peak months, as long as you're prepared for cooler temperatures and the possibility of rain.

Viana do Castelo is known for its festivals and events, so if your visit coincides with one of these, be sure to join in the celebrations. Some of the most popular events include the Festa de Nossa Senhora da Agonia in August, which features parades, folk dancing, and fireworks, and the Semana do Mar (Sea Week) in September, which celebrates the city's maritime heritage with boat races, music, and cultural activities.

No matter when you visit, Viana do Castelo offers a memorable day trip from Porto, filled with history, culture, and beautiful scenery.

## 3. Braga

Braga is a city located in northwestern Portugal. It is known as the "City of Churches" due to the large number of churches located within its city limits. Some of the most notable churches in Braga include the Cathedral of Braga, which was built in the 12th century, and the Church of Bom Jesus do Monte, which is known for its Baroque architecture. Braga is also home to a number of museums, including the Museum of Archeology, which houses a collection of artifacts from the Roman period.

**Day Trip Itinerary to Braga from Porto**

08:00 – Depart from Porto Start your day at São Bento Railway Station in Porto. Catch the train to Braga, which usually takes around 1 hour. Trains run frequently throughout the day, and you can check the schedule and ticket prices on the Comboios de Portugal website (https://www.cp.pt/).

09:00 – Arrive in Braga Upon arrival in Braga, take a few minutes to get your bearings and enjoy a quick coffee at a local café near the train station.

09:30 – Visit Braga Cathedral Begin your exploration of Braga at the city's historic cathedral, which dates back to the 12th century. Admire the mix of architectural styles, from Romanesque to Baroque, and visit the beautiful chapels and cloisters.

10:30 – Explore the Historic Center Stroll through Braga's picturesque historic center, taking in the charming streets, elegant squares, and stunning churches. Be sure to visit the iconic Arco da Porta Nova, a Baroque gateway that marks the entrance to the city.

11:30 – Church of Bom Jesus do Monte Take a bus or taxi to the Church of Bom Jesus do Monte, a remarkable sanctuary known for its Baroque stairway and beautiful gardens. You can also ride the Bom Jesus funicular, which is the oldest water-powered funicular in the world.

13:00 – Lunch Break Enjoy a leisurely lunch at a local restaurant, such as Cozinha da Se (https://www.facebook.com/cozinhadase/) or Bracara Augusta (https://www.bracaraaugusta.pt/), where you can savor traditional Portuguese cuisine.

14:30 – Visit the Garden of Santa Barbara After lunch, head to the Garden of Santa Barbara, a beautiful public garden featuring manicured hedges, colorful flowers, and a stunning fountain.

15:00 – Discover the Biscainhos Museum Visit the Biscainhos Museum, a charming museum housed in an 18th-century palace. The museum showcases decorative arts, ceramics, and furnishings, offering a glimpse into the lives of Braga's aristocracy.

16:00 – Church of São Martinho de Tibães Head to the Church of São Martinho de Tibães, a beautiful Baroque church with an impressive gold-leaf interior. Take some time to explore the church and its surrounding gardens.

17:00 – Free Time for Shopping and Exploration Spend the remainder of your afternoon exploring any areas you may have missed earlier, or indulge in some shopping at local boutiques and souvenir shops.

19:00 – Dinner in Braga Before heading back to Porto, enjoy a delicious dinner at a local restaurant, such as Restaurante Centurium (https://www.facebook.com/restaurante.centurium/) or Restaurante Dom Augusto (https://www.facebook.com/restaurantedomaugusto/).

20:30 – Depart from Braga Return to the Braga train station and catch a train back to Porto. Check the train schedule on the Comboios de Portugal website (https://www.cp.pt/).

21:30 – Arrive in Porto Arrive back in Porto, bringing your day trip to Braga to a close.

Note: The best time to visit Braga is between April and October when the weather is pleasant and mild. However, the city can be enjoyed year-round, with cooler temperatures and the possibility of rain during the winter months.

## 4. Aveiro

Aveiro is a city located in central Portugal. It is known as the "Venice of Portugal" due to its canals and bridges. The city is home to a number of landmarks, including the Church of Santo António, which was built in the 16th century, and the Aveiro Cathedral, which was built in the 18th century. Aveiro is also home to a number of museums, including the Museum of Aveiro, which houses a collection of artifacts from the city's history.

## 5. Coimbra

Coimbra is a city located in central Portugal, known for its rich history and stunning architecture. It is home to the University of Coimbra, one of the oldest universities in Europe, which was declared a UNESCO World Heritage Site in 2013. The city boasts several impressive landmarks, such as the Old Cathedral, the Monastery of Santa Cruz, and the Joanina Library. Coimbra also hosts various museums, including the Machado de Castro National Museum, which houses an extensive collection of sculptures, paintings, and other artifacts.

## 6. Douro Valley

The Douro Valley is a picturesque region in northern Portugal, famous for its terraced vineyards, winding river, and charming villages. As the heart of Portugal's wine country, the Douro Valley is an ideal destination for wine lovers who want to visit wineries, enjoy wine tastings, and explore the beautiful landscape. Take a scenic train ride, a relaxing river cruise, or a guided tour to experience the stunning beauty and unique flavors of this UNESCO World Heritage Site.

## 7. Peneda-Gerês National

Park Peneda-Gerês National Park, located in the northwest corner of Portugal, is the country's only national park. It features diverse landscapes, including forests, mountains, rivers, and waterfalls, making it a haven for nature enthusiasts and outdoor adventurers. Visitors can enjoy hiking, birdwatching, swimming in natural pools, or simply exploring the picturesque villages within the park. The park is also home to historical landmarks, such as the Castle of Lindoso and the Sanctuary of Nossa Senhora da Peneda.

## 8. Amarante

Amarante is a charming town in northern Portugal, nestled along the Tâmega River. It is known for its picturesque scenery, historic sites, and vibrant cultural events. Notable landmarks include the Church of São Gonçalo, the Bridge of São Gonçalo, and the Amadeo de Souza-Cardoso Museum, which showcases works by renowned Portuguese artists. Visitors can also enjoy leisurely strolls along the river, sample the famous pastries at Pão de Ló de Amarante, or participate in local festivals, such as the Festa de São Gonçalo.

# 9. Practical Information

## Getting There

### By Plane

Porto International Airport (OPO) is located 11km (6.8 miles) northwest o
the city center.

Aegean Airlines, Aer Lingus, Aeroflot, Air Canada, Air China, Air France,
Alitalia, British Airways, easyJet, Emirates, Iberia, KLM, Lufthansa,
Norwegian, Ryanair, Swiss, TAP Air Portugal, Turkish Airlines, United and
Vueling all fly direct to Porto.

If you're flying from the US, TAP Air Portugal offers the most convenient
direct flights, departing from Newark, New York JFK, Boston and Miami.

From the airport, you can reach the city center by taxi (around EUR 20-
25), by bus (EUR 3.50) or by metro (EUR 2).

### By Train

Porto's train station, Campanhã, is located about 2km (1.2 miles)
southeast of the city center.

There are direct trains to/from Lisbon (3 hours), Braga (1 hour), Coimbra
(2 hours), Guimarães (40 minutes), Aveiro (1 hour) and Viana do Castelo
(1.5 hours).

If you're coming from Spain, you can take a direct train from Madrid (8.5
hours) or from Barcelona (11 hours).

Alternatively, you can take a bus from Lisbon (4 hours) or from Braga (2
hours).

### By Bus

Porto's main bus station, Estação de Campanhã, is located about 2km (1.2
miles) southeast of the city center.

From Lisbon, there are direct buses to Porto (4 hours) and from Braga (2
hours).

If you're coming from Spain, you can take a direct bus from Madrid (9 hours) or from Barcelona (11 hours).

**By Car**

Porto is located about midway between Lisbon (280km/174 miles) and the Spanish border (300km/186 miles).

If you're driving from Lisbon, take the A1 motorway north. If you're driving from Spain, take the A3 motorway south.

## 9.1 The Monthly Weather in Porto

The climate in Porto is Mediterranean, with mild, rainy winters and hot, dry summers. The average temperature in January is 12.5 degrees Celsius, and in July it is 26.5 degrees Celsius. The average annual rainfall is 1,207 millimeters.

The best time to visit Porto is from April to June, or from September to October. These months offer the most pleasant weather, with average temperatures of 16-18 degrees Celsius. July and August are the hottest months, with temperatures often reaching 30 degrees Celsius or higher. November to March is the rainy season, so visitors should be prepared for some wet weather if they travel during these months.

## 9.2 Helpful Local Phrases

In Porto, as in any other city, it is always helpful to know a few local phrases to make your way around. Below are 9.3 helpful local phrases in Porto that will surely come in handy during your visit:

1. Obrigado/a - Thank you

2. Por favor - Please

3. Desculpe - Excuse me/I'm sorry

4. Como vai? - How are you?

5. Quanto custa? - How much does it cost?

6. Onde fica? - Where is it?

7. Boa noite - Good evening

8. Boa tarde - Good afternoon

9. Adeus - Goodbye

With these few local phrases, you will be able to get by in Porto with ease. Be sure to practice them before your visit so that you can hit the ground running and make the most of your time in this wonderful city.

## 9.3 Money and Budget

Portugal's second-largest city, Porto is a charming destination with plenty to see and do. Although it can be expensive, there are ways to save money and stick to a budget while enjoying everything this historic city has to offer.

Portugal is a relatively inexpensive country to visit, but Porto is one of the more expensive cities. The average daily cost for a traveler is about $100, which includes accommodation, food, transportation, and activities.

To save money on accommodation, consider staying in a hostel or an Airbnb. Hostels in Porto start at around $15 per night, and Airbnbs can be found for as little as $30 per night. For food, take advantage of the many affordable eateries serving up delicious Portuguese cuisine. Street food is also a great option, and you can find a meal for as little as $5.

When it comes to transportation, walking is the best way to get around Porto. If you need to use public transportation, a 24-hour pass is only $5. For activities, take advantage of the free walking tours, visit the many museums (most have free admission on Sundays), and enjoy the city's scenic views.

With a little planning, it is possible to visit Porto on a budget and still have a great time.

## 9.4 Safety and Emergency Contacts

In the case of an emergency, always call 112.

For non-urgent medical assistance, you can call the following numbers:

- SOS Médicos: 808 200 520
- Serviço de Urgência Básico: 808 247 424

For firefighters, you can call the following number:

- Bombeiros Voluntários do Porto: 225 059 699

For the police, you can call the following number:

Polícia de Segurança Pública: 253 617 617

If you need legal assistance, you can contact the following number:

Association of Portuguese Lawyers: 226 059649

## 9.5 Contact Details of the Main Embassies

The following is a list of the main embassies located in Porto:

**Australia:**

Avenida dos Aliados, 25-27, 4000-038 Porto, Phone: +351 22 339 3900, Fax: +351 22 339 3999, Email: portugal.embassy@dfat.gov.au

**Canada:**

Rua Cândido Landolt, 2300-315, 4200-132 Porto, Phone: +351 22 993 3000, Fax: +351 22 993 3099, Email: portugal.consulate@international.gc.ca

**France:**

Rua António Maria Cardoso, 38, 4050-347 Porto, Phone: +351 22 5081800, Fax: +351 22 5081801, Email: france.porto@diplomatie.gouv.fr

**Germany:**

Edifício Vodafone, Rua D. João IV, nº1, 5º , 4100-313 Porto, Phone: +351 22 339 3900, Fax: +351 22 339 3999, Email: info@porto.diplo.de

**Ireland:**

Rua do Almada, 216-4º , 4000-290 Porto, Phone: +351 22 200 8200, Fax: +351 22 200 8201, Email: porto@dfa.ie

**Netherlands:**

Avenida da Boavista, 1565 - 4º, 4100-137 Porto, Phone: +351 22 508 5800, Fax: +351 22 508 5801, Email: por@minbuza.nl

**United Kingdom:**

Rua Mouzinho da Silveira, 182/184, 4000-417 Porto, Phone: +351 22 339 3900, Fax: +351 22 339 3999, Email: porto.consulate@fco.gov.uk

**United States:**

Rua da Imprensa Nacional, 1 , 1250-191 Lisboa, Phone: +351 217272727, Fax: +351 218117417

## 9.6 General Tips on Porto

Here are some general tips to help you make the most of your visit to Porto:

1. Get lost in the atmospheric Old Town: Porto's Old Town is a UNESCO World Heritage Site and one of the city's most atmospheric and charming areas. Stroll through the narrow streets and alleyways, admire the traditional azulejo tiles, and soak up the unique atmosphere.

2. Visit the Palacio da Bolsa: Porto's Palacio da Bolsa is one of the city's most iconic and impressive buildings. Built in the 19th century, it was once the stock exchange, and today it houses a cultural centre. Visitors can admire the opulent interiors and learn about the building's history on a guided tour.

3. Take a cruise on the Douro River: A cruise on the Douro River is one of the best ways to see Porto's stunning riverfront. There are a number of different cruise options available, ranging from short sightseeing cruises to longer dinner cruises.

4. Sample the local port wine: Porto is famous for its port wine, and there are a number of ways to sample this delicious tipple. Visit one of the

many port wine lodges in the city, go on a port wine tour, or simply enjoy a glass or two in one of Porto's many bars and restaurants.

5. Visit the Sao Bento Railway Station: Porto's Sao Bento Railway Station is one of the city's most iconic landmarks. Built in the early 20th century, it is famous for its beautiful azulejo tiles, which depict scenes from Portuguese history.

6.Explore the Serralves Foundation: The Serralves Foundation is a must-visit for anyone interested in contemporary art. The foundation houses a museum, an art gallery, and a sculpture park, set in 18 hectares of lush gardens.

7. Take a day trip to the beach: Porto may be inland, but that doesn't mean you can't enjoy some time at the beach. The city's coastal suburbs, such as Matosinhos, Foz do Douro, and Miramar, offer beautiful sandy beaches and lively waterfront promenades. Take a bus or tram from the city center, and you'll be at the beach in no time.

8. Wander through Ribeira: This UNESCO World Heritage site is the oldest neighborhood in Porto. Stroll along its narrow cobblestone streets, admire the colorful houses, and enjoy the vibrant atmosphere of its many cafes, restaurants, and bars.

9. Visit Livraria Lello: Known as one of the most beautiful bookstores in the world, Livraria Lello has been inspiring book lovers since 1906. Its stunning neo-Gothic architecture, including a magnificent red staircase, makes it a must-visit attraction.

10. Sample Portuguese cuisine: Porto's food scene is renowned for its delicious dishes, such as francesinha, bacalhau, and pastel de nata. Visit the historic Bolhão Market for fresh produce and local delicacies, or dine at one of the city's many fantastic restaurants.

11. Attend a fado performance: Experience the soulful sounds of fado, Portugal's traditional music genre. Numerous venues across the city offer intimate performances, allowing you to immerse yourself in this hauntingly beautiful musical tradition.

12. Go wine tasting in the Douro Valley: A visit to Porto wouldn't be complete without exploring the nearby Douro Valley, the birthplace of port wine. Take a day trip to the valley and visit some of the

region's best wineries, where you can learn about the winemaking process and sample some of the finest port wines.

13. Climb the Clérigos Tower: For a stunning panoramic view of Porto, climb the 225 steps to the top of the Clérigos Tower. This iconic baroque tower offers breathtaking vistas of the city and the Douro River.

14. Discover the Palácio da Bolsa: This impressive 19th-century building was once the city's stock exchange. Today, it is a cultural center and event venue, with guided tours available to explore its ornate architecture and rich history.

## 9.8 Useful Mobile Apps to Download for your trip to Porto

There are many mobile apps that can be useful for visitors to Porto. Here are a few of the most useful ones:

1. Visit Porto (Official Travel Guide) - An official app developed by the city of Porto. It provides useful information about attractions, museums, restaurants, and events. Get recommendations for itineraries, guided tours, and public transport options.

2. Porto Card - This app is perfect for tourists planning to visit multiple attractions. It allows you to purchase and manage the Porto Card, which offers discounts and free admission to popular attractions and museums, as well as discounts on public transportation.

3. Metro do Porto - Navigating Porto's public transport system is made easy with this app. Access detailed information on metro lines, schedules, and ticket prices, and find the nearest metro station based on your location.

4. STCP - This app covers Porto's bus network, providing real-time information about routes, stops, and schedules. It also offers a trip planner feature that helps you find the best way to get from one place to another using buses.

5. Uber - While public transportation in Porto is efficient, Uber can be a convenient option for getting around the city. This app allows you to request rides, track your driver, and pay for your trip through your smartphone.

6. MyTaxi - This app connects you with local taxis in Porto. With MyTaxi, you can easily book a taxi, track its arrival, and pay for your ride through the app.

7. Time Out Porto - Stay updated on events, concerts, and festivals happening in the city during your visit. This app provides information on Porto's cultural scene, including art exhibitions, theater shows, and food events.

8. Zomato - Discover the best restaurants, cafes, and bars in Porto with this app. Browse user reviews, check menus, and make reservations for dining experiences that suit your taste.

9. Speak & Translate - While many locals in Porto speak English, having a translation app can be useful. Speak & Translate allows you to translate text and voice messages between English and Portuguese, making it easier to communicate with locals and understand signs and menus.

10. Wi-Fi Finder - Stay connected while exploring Porto with this app that helps you locate free Wi-Fi hotspots around the city. Browse an interactive map to find the nearest Wi-Fi spot and get directions to reach it.

## 9.9 Capturing Porto's Beauty: A Guide to the Most Photogenic Spots in the City

Porto, the enchanting city in Northern Portugal, is a photographer's dream with its colorful buildings, stunning viewpoints, and historic landmarks. In this guide, we'll explore some of the most photogenic spots in Porto, perfect for capturing unforgettable memories of your visit.

1. Ribeira District The Ribeira District, a UNESCO World Heritage Site, is the heart of Porto's old town. With its narrow cobblestone streets, vibrant houses, and charming squares, Ribeira offers a picturesque backdrop for your photos. Don't miss the iconic view of the Douro River, Dom Luís I Bridge, and the colorful houses along the waterfront.

2. Dom Luís I Bridge The Dom Luís I Bridge, an iron double-deck bridge, is not only a crucial transportation link but also a fantastic spot to capture panoramic views of Porto. Head to the upper deck for a

breathtaking vantage point of the city, the Douro River, and the Ribeira District.

3. Clérigos Tower Climb the 225 steps to the top of the Clérigos Tower, one of Porto's most iconic landmarks, and enjoy sweeping views of the city. The Baroque-style tower and its surrounding buildings make for a striking subject in your photographs.

4. Livraria Lello The enchanting Livraria Lello is one of the world's most beautiful bookstores. Capture the essence of its stunning architecture, featuring intricate wooden details, a vibrant red staircase, and a stunning stained-glass skylight.

5. Crystal Palace Gardens For a tranquil escape, head to the Crystal Palace Gardens, which offers not only lush greenery but also panoramic views of the Douro River and Porto's skyline. The park's various viewpoints and the romantic atmosphere make it an ideal spot for photography.

6. São Bento Train Station São Bento Train Station is a true masterpiece, adorned with over 20,000 azulejo tiles that depict scenes from Portuguese history. Capture the intricate tilework and the station's beautiful architecture in your photos.

7. Foz do Douro Foz do Douro, where the Douro River meets the Atlantic Ocean, offers stunning coastal views and beautiful beaches. The Felgueiras Lighthouse and the Pergola da Foz are particularly photogenic spots in this area.

8. Serralves Museum and Park The Serralves Museum, a contemporary art museum, and its surrounding park provide a modern and artistic backdrop for your photographs. The minimalist architecture of the museum, the beautiful gardens, and the unique sculptures throughout the park make for a visually captivating experience.

9. Palácio de Cristal Gardens Another picturesque garden in Porto, the Palácio de Cristal Gardens, offers beautiful greenery, peacock sightings, and panoramic views of the Douro River. The romantic pathways and the iconic domed pavilion make for beautiful photo opportunities.

10. Porto Cathedral (Sé do Porto) The Porto Cathedral, a historic Romanesque and Gothic-style church, offers not only an impressive architectural subject but also fantastic views of the city from its terrace.

# Porto Classic: A 3-day itinerary for first-timers

**Day 1: Arrival, Top Monuments**

**09:45**

Arrive at Francisco Sá Carneiro Airport (Oporto International Airport), located 12 km north of Porto city center. As the second largest airport in Portugal, it has been consistently ranked in the Top 3 for Best Airport in Europe since 2006, even winning the award in 2007.

**09:55**

Collect your luggage and pass through passport control. If you're traveling with hand luggage only, it usually takes no more than 3 to 5 minutes to reach the arrivals terminal.

**10:05**

Take the metro, bus, or shuttle from the airport to the city center and check in to your hotel, MyStay Porto (or other hotel you may choose). Visit the official Porto public transport website (https://www.stcp.pt/en/travel/) for more information on schedules and ticket prices. COSTS: Metro: 1.85€ + 0.60€ for Andante Card (rechargeable) (35 minutes) Bus: 1.85€ (50 minutes) Taxi: 25€-30€ (25 minutes)

**11:20**

After settling into your hotel, begin your exploration of Porto's top monuments, all within walking distance. Start with Clérigos Tower (https://www.torredosclerigos.pt/) and the Portuguese Center of Photography (http://www.cpf.pt/). COSTS: Clérigos Tower Ticket Price: 3€ Portuguese Photography Center Ticket Price: Free

**14:00**

Lunch at Café Santiago (https://cafesantiago.pt/), Rua Passos Manuel, 266, 4000-382 Porto. Tel: (+351) 22 205 5797. Known for their traditional francesinha, this restaurant is a must-visit. Be prepared to wait for a table, but the experience is well worth it. COST: 12€-14€ per person

**15:30**

Visit the Bolhão Market (https://www.bolhaomarket.pt/en/), Porto's famous traditional market, offering fresh fish, vegetables, and fruits. Ticket Price: Free

**18:00**

Stroll along Aliados Avenue or shop at Santa Catarina Street, two bustling and commercial streets in Porto. Relax at one of the many cafes lining the avenue, but be aware of pickpockets in crowded areas.

**20:00**

Dine in the Ribeira area, where you'll find an array of appealing restaurants. If you're interested, try the grilled sardines for dinner, while enjoying stunning views of the D. Luis Bridge. You can find various options on the Porto Restaurant Guide website (https://porto-north.travel/restaurant-guide/). COST: 10€ per person.

**22:00**

Return to your hotel and rest up for the next day's adventures.

## 1st Day in Porto Map

The "1st Day in Porto Map" is a specially curated Google Map designed to help you navigate your first day in Porto with ease. This interactive map (https://www.google.com/maps/d/edit?mid=zg5djDmJ6KII.kCB_UUBcM mdl&usp=sharing) features all the essential locations and points of interest mentioned in the Day 1 itinerary, providing a visual guide for your journey through Porto. From your arrival at Francisco Sá Carneiro Airport to visiting iconic monuments, indulging in delicious meals, and exploring popular streets, this map ensures that you can easily locate each destination and plan your day efficiently, making the most of your time in this enchanting city.

## ZoomTip 1.1 Transportation and ATMs

There are various ways to get to the city center. It depends on the amount you can afford. I usually took the **metro**, but once I took the bus, due to a late arrivael. There are different operating hours, depending on the transportation mean.

The options from Francisco Sá Carneiro Airport to the city center are:

- **Taxi:** about 20- 30€ to Avenida dos Aliados (approximately: 25min). Rates go up by 20% in the evening hours, as from 9pm to 6am.

- **Metro:**

Clearly the easiest way to get into Oporto city center. Just follow the information displayed in the arrivals terminal and you'll reach the Metro very fast. Buy an Andante Card (0,60€), which will be your transportation card for the next few days and every time you come to Oporto. Then, select a ticket Z4 (Zone 4) which will cost 1,85€. The Andante Card, as well as the metro single journey tickets, can be bought on the machines near the Airport Metro Station. Line E (Purple), direction Estádio do Dragão. Stop at Trindade and take a connection with Line D (Yellow) and stop at São Bento (approximately: 35min). Just walk from the São Bento Station to your hotel, which will take 10 to 15min.

- **The public bus** (Lines 601, 602, 604 and 3M).

Each ticket costs 1,85€ and the journey will take 1h to 1h10min. To reach your hotel, the best option are clearly Lines 601 and 602, given the fact that *Cordoaria* (final bus stop) is only a 5min walk from your hotel.


**ZoomTip 1.2: Information on the Monuments**

**Clérigos Tower and Church**

**Info:** With remarkable panoramic views over the Douro river and the entire city of Oporto, the Clérigos Tower rises up 75,6 meters from the ground, being the tallest bell tower in the entire country. Dating back from the 1 18th-century, this baroque style structure is one of the most recognizable and iconic buildings of the city.

**Hours:** 9am to 7pm (except 24, 25, 31 December and 1 January).

**Ticket Price**: 3€.

**Portuguese Photography Center**

**Info:** Created in 1997, this art center is located in a historic building that served as a prison until 1974. Some famous Portuguese criminals ,like Camilo Castelo Branco , were once incarcerated in this late 18th-century building. Nowadays, you'll find the previous cells completely refurnished with photography materials, just like a museum, as well as some of the finest Portuguese photography art collection.

**Hours:** 10am to 6pm (Tuesday to Friday), 3pm to 7pm (Saturday to Sunday). Closed on Monday.

**Ticket Price**: Free

## Bolhão Market

**Info:** Dating back from 1839, this is the most emblematic market of the city, probably the only place where you'll find (and meet) typical and traditional inhabitants of this lovely city.

**Hours:** 7am to 5pm (Monday to Firday), 7am to 1pm (Saturday). Closed on Sunday.

**Ticket Price**: Free

### ZoomTip 1.3: Eat the Famous Francesinha

Every restaurant, bar or cafe in Oporto has its own *francesinha*. It's a "sandwinch" type dish, since it has bread underneath and on top. However, the filling has a large variety of ham's, "*enchido's*" and meat. A fried egg on top of the cheese is one of the best parts of this dish. The difference-maker that turns a good *francesinha* into an outstanding one is the sauce, and Café Santiago keeps its secret for decades!

### Café Santiago

Passos Manuel Street, 226 (in front of *Coliseu do Porto*), 4000-382 Oporto, Tel: (00351) 22 205 5797, Website: www.caferestaurantesantiago.com.pt

### Café Santiago F

Passos Manuel Street, 198 (in front of *Coliseu do Porto*), 4000-382 Oporto, Tel: (00351) 22 205 5797, Website: www.caferestaurantesantiago.com.pt

## Day 2: Douro Cruise and Nearby attractions

**09:30**

### Six bridge cruise over Douro River + Port wine tasting Tour

Time to enjoy what the best that Oporto has to offer.: A river cruise. Buy your ticket in many of the tourists points that you'll find in the city center. There's one or two shops selling this tickets near the Aliados Avenue and São Bento Station.

Buy a ticket that includes the six bridge cruise + port wine tasting or six bridge cruise + port wine tasting + touristic train. The touristic train is something you'll find everywhere. However, there's nothing like a cruise in a river like the calm and relaxing Douro.

Don't forget to have your camera ready, since the views to the *Cais da Ribeira* or *Cais de Gaia* are simply stunning! There's no better way to enjoy a sunny morning in of Europe's most wonderful cities.

Note: you'll be departing from *Cais da Ribeira*.

COSTS: Depends on the company you choose (Average: 15€)

**11:45**

### Visit the *São Francisco* Church and *Palácio da Bolsa* (Stock Exchange Palace)

They are both near *Cais da Ribeira*, where your cruise ended, so you don't need to walk that much.

View *ZoomTip 2.1*

### *COSTS:*

*São Francisco* Church Ticket Price: Free

*Palácio da Bolsa* Ticket Price: 7,50€ (students: 4€)

**13:45**

**Lunch at *Cais de Gaia***

One the other margin of the river, just in front of *Cais da Ribeira* where you had dinner yesterday, there's another area full of restaurants, bars and traditional pubs. I recommend you to lunch at Rebelos, where the cod is simply delicious! Also, very complete list of wines.

COSTS: Depends on what you choose (Average: 15€-20€)

**Day 2: Cathedral of Oporto, Dinner and Bars**

**16:00 - Explore the Porto Cathedral (Sé do Porto)**

After a delightful meal, enjoy a leisurely walk to the São Bento Train Station. From there, you will spot the impressive Porto Cathedral just a few hundred meters away. This historic cathedral, dating back to the 12th century, is a must-see attraction for every visitor. Admire the stunning Romanesque and Gothic architecture and the beautiful rose window. Visit the church's official website for more information on guided tours and special events: http://www.diocese-porto.pt/.

Ticket price: Church (free), Cloisters (3€).

**18:00 - Indulge at Majestic Café**

Treat yourself to a luxurious break at Majestic Café, the most famous and elegant café in the heart of Porto. Although it's slightly pricier than other coffee shops, the exquisite ambiance and historical charm make it worth the visit. Enjoy a selection of pastries, sandwiches, and beverages amidst the ornate décor. Visit their website for more information: https://www.cafemajestic.com/en. Costs: Depending on your selection.

**20:00 - Savor Dinner at Tasca Caseira**

Experience traditional Portuguese cuisine at Tasca Caseira, where you can enjoy a wide variety of delicious dishes at a reasonable price. The restaurant offers a tapas-style menu, allowing you to sample various flavors and dishes. Each plate is carefully crafted, ensuring a memorable dining experience. Check their Facebook page for updates and menu options: https://www.facebook.com/Tasca-Caseira-1686945068229193/. Costs: 10€ - 15€ per person.

### 22:00 - Unwind at a Bar in Galerias de Paris

 End your evening at Galerias de Paris, a bustling nightlife area in Porto, just a 5-minute walk from your hotel. The district offers an array of bars and pubs, ensuring you'll find the perfect spot to relax and enjoy a drink. Whether you prefer a laid-back atmosphere or a lively venue, Galerias de Paris has something for everyone. Costs: Depends on your drink selection

### Porto 2nd Day Map

Oporto 2nd Day Map: https://www.google.com/maps/d/edit?mid=zg5djDmJ6KII.kQH5cl9DCj2I&usp=sharing

### ZoomTip 1.2: Information on the Monuments

### São Francisco Church

**Info:** This gothic style church is one of the most amazing examples of this architecture style in Portugal. Dating back from 1425, it was declared as a World Heritage Site by UNESCO., as a part of the historic city center of Oporto Don't miss the stunning interior with a baroque decoration. The view towards the main chapel will worth the trip.

**Hours:** 9am to 5:30pm (Nov-Feb), 9am to 7pm (Mar-Oct), 9am to 8pm (Jul-Sep).| **Ticket Price**: Free


### Palácio da Bolsa (Stock Exchange Palace)

**Info:** This 19th-century palace was built by the City's Commercial Association and is a part of the historical centre of Oporto, which was consecrated as a World Heritage Site by UNESCO. The various luxurious rooms makes this building one of the most touristic sights of the city.

**Hours:** 9am to 6:30pm (Apr-Oct), 9am to 12:30pm / 2:30pm to 5:30pm (Nov-Mar)|**Ticket Price**: 7,50€ (students: 4€)


### Cathedral of Oporto

**Info:** With a gorgeous façade and dating back from 1737, this building is of the oldest monuments in Oporto. Its construction began in the 12th-century, but some modifications had happened since then. A truly must-see for every tourist visiting this lovely city!

**Hours:** 9am to 7pm.

**Ticket Price**: Church (free), Cloisters (3€).


### Day 3: Museum's Day

### 09:00 - Explore the National Museum Soares dos Reis

 Begin your day at the National Museum Soares dos Reis, showcasing a diverse collection of Portuguese art from the 16th to the 20th century. Take bus lines 601 or 602 from Cordoaria, located near your hotel, or enjoy a 10-minute stroll to the museum. Visit their website for more information on current exhibitions and events: http://mnsr.imc-ip.pt/. Ticket Price: 5€ (students: 2.5€)

### 11:00 - Stroll through the Crystal Palace Gardens

Just 300 meters away, you'll find the enchanting Crystal Palace Gardens (Jardins do Palácio de Cristal). Wander through the lush greenery while admiring Porto's stunning architecture and take in the breathtaking views of the Douro River. Remember to bring your camera for capturing memorable moments. Admission: Free

### 13:00 - Lunch Break at Capa Negra II Restaurant

Savor a delicious lunch at Capa Negra II, known for serving one of Porto's best francesinhas. If you prefer other options, their diverse menu offers a wide variety of tasty dishes to choose from. Address: Rua Campo Alegre, 191 Timetable: 12 pm to 2 am Website: http://www.capanegra.com/ Costs: 12€ - 15€ per person

### 15:00 - Admire Casa da Música

After lunch, continue your walk to Casa da Música, a world-renowned concert hall celebrated for its spectacular modern architecture. Learn about upcoming performances and events on their website: https://www.casadamusica.com/.

### 15:30 - Visit the Serralves Foundation

A short stroll down Boavista Avenue brings you to the Serralves Foundation, one of Portugal's most prestigious museums. Discover contemporary art and culture at this must-visit attraction. For more information, visit their website: https://www.serralves.pt/. Ticket Price: 8.5€

### 18:00 - Explore Queijo Castle and Foz Area

Return to Boavista Avenue and catch a bus to the end of the avenue, where the historic Queijo Castle stands. Stroll along the picturesque Foz area, a favorite spot for locals to enjoy the sunset with stunning views of the Atlantic Ocean. This relaxing walk is the perfect way to rejuvenate after a busy day.

### 19:30 - Return to the Hotel

Head back to the hotel and unwind. You may want to consider taking a taxi for added convenience, which will cost approximately 5€.

### 20:30 - Dinner at Cais da Ribeira

End your day with a delightful dinner at Cais da Ribeira, overlooking the beautiful Dom Luís I Bridge. Choose from a variety of restaurants offering delicious cuisine to suit your appetite. Cost: 10€-15€ per person

## 23:00 - Return to the Hotel

Get some rest in preparation for your early flight the next day.

## Porto 3d Day Map

Porto 3rd Day Map:
https://www.google.com/maps/d/edit?mid=zg5djDmJ6KII.kPXPYxQ0yIsE&usp=sharing

# Porto's Historical Highlights: A 2-Day Itinerary for History Buffs

**Day 1:**

08:00 - Breakfast Start your day with a hearty breakfast at a local café or bakery. One great option is Confeitaria do Bolhão (http://www.confeitariadobolhao.com/), a historic bakery in Porto, known for its delicious pastries and warm atmosphere.

09:00 - São Bento Railway Station Visit the São Bento Railway Station, a stunning building known for its intricate azulejo tile panels depicting historical scenes from Portugal's past. This architectural masterpiece is a must-see for history lovers. More information: http://www.visitporto.travel/Visitar/Paginas/Descobrir/DetalhesPoi.aspx?POI=1232

10:00 - Clérigos Church and Tower Next, head to the Clérigos Church and Tower. Climb the iconic Baroque tower for panoramic views of the city and learn about the church's history. Admission: €6 (includes access to the church, tower, and museum). Official website: http://www.torredosclerigos.pt/en/

11:30 - Livraria Lello Visit Livraria Lello, one of the most beautiful bookstores in the world, known for its stunning architecture and historical significance. There is a €5 entry fee, but it is redeemable against any book purchase. More information: https://www.livrarialello.pt/en_US/

12:30 - Lunch Enjoy a traditional Portuguese lunch at Restaurante Trasca (https://www.facebook.com/trascarestaurante/), a cozy and authentic restaurant located in the heart of Porto.

14:00 - Porto Cathedral (Sé do Porto) Explore the Porto Cathedral, a 12th-century Romanesque church with a fascinating history. Don't forget to visit the Gothic cloisters adorned with beautiful azulejo tiles. Admission to the church is free, but the cloisters have a €3 entrance fee. More information: http://www.visitporto.travel/Visitar/Paginas/Descobrir/DetalhesPoi.aspx?POI=1240

15:30 - Church of Saint Francis (Igreja de São Francisco) Visit the Church of Saint Francis, an impressive Gothic church known for its ornate Baroque interior and intricate wood carvings. Admission: €7.50 (includes access to the church, catacombs, and museum). Official website: https://www.visitportugal.com/en/NR/exeres/34B290E8-8BAA-4DCE-91CD-7C8BA3D2C592

17:00 - Ribeira District Spend the late afternoon exploring the Ribeira District, a UNESCO World Heritage Site with narrow streets, colorful houses, and charming squares. Relax at a local café or browse the shops in the area.

19:00 - Dinner For dinner, try Adega São Nicolau (https://www.facebook.com/AdegaSaoNicolau), a traditional Portuguese restaurant known for its delicious food and welcoming atmosphere.

21:00 - Evening stroll along the Douro River After dinner, take a leisurely evening walk along the Douro River, admiring the stunning views of the Dom Luís I Bridge and the city's skyline.

23:00 - Return to accommodation

**Day 2:**

08:00 - Breakfast Start your day with breakfast at a local café, such as Nata Lisboa (https://natalisboa.pt/), which is known for its pastéis de nata and other delicious pastries.

09:00 - Palácio da Bolsa Visit the Palácio da Bolsa, a 19th-century neoclassical building that was once the city's stock exchange. Explore its lavishly decorated rooms, including the famous Arab Room. Admission: €10. Official website: https://www.palaciodabolsa.com/

10:30 - Church of Santa Clara (Igreja de Santa Clara) Discover the hidden gem of Porto, the Church of Santa Clara, a beautiful example of Manueline and Baroque architecture. Its intricate wood carvings and gold leaf details make it a must-see for history enthusiasts. Admission: Free.

11:30 - Serralves Museum and Gardens Head to the Serralves Museum and Gardens, a modern art museum set within a beautiful park. The museum showcases contemporary art and the surrounding gardens are perfect for a leisurely walk. Admission: €12 (includes access to the museum, villa, and park). Official website: https://www.serralves.pt/en/

13:30 - Lunch Enjoy lunch at Casa de Pasto da Palmeira (https://www.facebook.com/Casa-de-Pasto-da-Palmeira-391264900970086/), a charming restaurant with delicious Portuguese cuisine and a relaxed atmosphere.

15:00 - Soares dos Reis National Museum Visit the Soares dos Reis National Museum, which houses an extensive collection of Portuguese art, sculpture, and decorative arts from the 19th and 20th centuries. Admission: €5 (students: €2.5). More information: http://www.visitporto.travel/Visitar/Paginas/Descobrir/DetalhesPoi.aspx?POI=1615

17:00 - Jardins do Palácio de Cristal Take a stroll through the Jardins do Palácio de Cristal, a beautiful park with stunning views of the Douro River and the city of Porto. Don't forget your camera! Admission: Free.

19:00 - Dinner Experience a traditional Portuguese dinner at Tapabento (http://www.tapabento.com/), a popular restaurant that offers a variety of tapas-style dishes made with fresh, local ingredients.

21:00 - Fado Show End your day with a captivating Fado show at Casa da Mariquinhas (https://www.casadamariquinhas.pt/), a famous Fado house in Porto. Immerse yourself in the soulful music and experience a piece of Portuguese culture. Show and dinner packages are available, starting at €30 per person.

23:00 - Return to accommodation

# Porto Food and Wine Tour: A Culinary Adventure in 3 Days

**Day 1:**

08:00 - Breakfast Start your culinary adventure in Porto with a delicious breakfast at Confeitaria do Bolhão (https://www.facebook.com/confeitariadobolhao/), a popular pastry shop known for its traditional Portuguese pastries, such as pastéis de nata and bola de Berlim.

09:30 - Bolhão Market Visit the bustling Bolhão Market, where you can explore the colorful stalls filled with fresh fruits, vegetables, fish, and other local products. Don't forget to try some of the local cheese and cured meats.

11:00 - Livraria Lello Take a break from food and visit Livraria Lello (https://www.livrarialello.pt/), one of the world's most beautiful bookstores, for some inspiration.

12:30 - Lunch at Café Santiago Head to Café Santiago (https://www.cafesantiago.pt/) for lunch and savor their famous francesinha, a hearty Porto sandwich layered with various meats and covered in a rich tomato and beer sauce.

14:30 - Wine Tasting at Caves Cálem Embark on a guided tour of the Caves Cálem (https://www.calem.pt/en), one of Porto's renowned port wine cellars, and indulge in a tasting of their delicious port wines.

16:30 - Explore the Ribeira District Spend some time wandering through the picturesque Ribeira District, stopping at local shops and tasting local delicacies like bolinhos de bacalhau (codfish cakes).

19:00 - Dinner at Cantinho do Avillez Treat yourself to a gourmet dinner at Cantinho do Avillez (https://www.cantinhodoavillez.pt/), a modern Portuguese restaurant by renowned chef José Avillez.

21:30 - Evening stroll along the Douro River After dinner, take a leisurely evening walk along the Douro River, admiring the stunning views of the Dom Luís I Bridge and the city's skyline.

23:00 - Return to accommodation

**Day 2:**

08:00 - Breakfast at Nata Lisboa Begin your day with breakfast at Nata Lisboa (https://natalisboa.pt/), where you can enjoy their famous pastéis de nata and other delicious pastries.

09:30 - Visit to Queijaria Amaral Discover the world of Portuguese cheese at Queijaria Amaral (http://www.queijariaamaral.com/), a cheese shop offering a wide variety of local and international cheeses. Enjoy a cheese tasting and learn about the different flavors and textures.

11:00 - Portuguese Coffee Experience Learn about the art of Portuguese coffee at a local café, such as Café Progresso (https://www.facebook.com/cafeprogresso), and enjoy a cup of the famous "café com cheirinho."

12:30 - Lunch at O Paparico Experience a traditional Portuguese lunch at O Paparico (http://www.opaparico.com/), a cozy restaurant that serves delicious, authentic dishes.

15:00 - Cooking Class Participate in a cooking class to learn how to prepare traditional Portuguese dishes with a local chef. Porto Food Tours (https://portofoodtours.com/) offers a variety of classes to choose from.

19:00 - Dinner at Pedro Lemos Indulge in a gourmet dinner at Pedro Lemos (http://www.pedrolemos.net/), a Michelin-starred restaurant that showcases the best of modern Portuguese cuisine.

22:00 - Drinks at Wine Quay Bar End the evening with a glass of local wine at Wine Quay Bar (https://www.facebook.com/winequaybarporto), a trendy waterfront bar with an extensive selection of Portuguese wines and a stunning view of the Douro River.

23:00 - Return to accommodation

**Day 3:**

08:00 - Breakfast at Molete Bread & Breakfast Start your day with a scrumptious breakfast at Molete Bread & Breakfast (https://www.facebook.com/moletebreadandbreakfast/), a charming bakery offering a variety of breads, pastries, and sandwiches.

10:00 - Guided Food Tour Embark on a guided food tour with Taste Porto (https://www.tasteporto.com/) to explore the city's culinary scene, sample local dishes, and learn about the history and culture of Porto's food.

14:00 - Lunch at Taberna dos Mercadores Enjoy a leisurely lunch at Taberna dos Mercadores (http://www.tabernadosmercadores.com/), a small, traditional restaurant known for its delicious seafood dishes and friendly service.

16:00 - Visit to Espaço Porto Cruz Discover the world of port wine at Espaço Porto Cruz (https://www.espacoportocruz.pt/), a modern wine center that offers tastings, workshops, and exhibitions about the history and production of this iconic drink.

18:30 - Aperitif at BASE Unwind with an aperitif and some light snacks at BASE (https://www.facebook.com/baseporto/), a trendy outdoor bar located in a beautiful garden setting.

20:00 - Dinner at Casa de Pasto da Palmeira Savor your final dinner in Porto at Casa de Pasto da Palmeira (https://www.facebook.com/casadepastodapalmeira/), a stylish eatery offering contemporary Portuguese cuisine made with locally sourced ingredients.

22:00 - Nightcap at Gin House End your culinary adventure with a nightcap at Gin House (https://www.facebook.com/ginhouseporto/), a cozy bar specializing in gin cocktails and offering a wide selection of Portuguese and international gins.

23:00 - Return to accommodation

# The Art Lover's Guide to Porto: A 4-Day Cultural Exploration

**Day 1:**

08:00 - Breakfast at Confeitaria do Bolhão Start your day with a delicious breakfast at Confeitaria do Bolhão (https://www.facebook.com/ConfeitariaBolhao), a historic pastry shop known for its traditional Portuguese pastries.

09:30 - Serralves Museum and Park Begin your cultural exploration with a visit to Serralves Museum (https://www.serralves.pt/en/), a contemporary art museum featuring works by national and international artists. After exploring the museum, take a leisurely stroll through the beautiful Serralves Park, located on the same grounds. To get there, take bus line 502 from Aliados to the Serralves stop.

13:00 - Lunch at Casa Guedes Enjoy a traditional Portuguese lunch at Casa Guedes (https://www.facebook.com/Casa-Guedes-733701230008558), famous for its mouthwatering pork sandwiches.

14:30 - Soares dos Reis National Museum Visit Soares dos Reis National Museum (http://mnsr.imc-ip.pt/), which houses a vast collection of Portuguese art from the 19th and 20th centuries. The museum is a 20-minute walk or a short bus ride (take bus line 202) from Casa Guedes.

17:00 - Galeria Presença Explore Galeria Presença (https://www.galeriapresenca.pt/), a contemporary art gallery showcasing works by emerging and established Portuguese artists. The gallery is a 15-minute walk from Soares dos Reis National Museum.

19:00 - Dinner at Cantinho do Avillez Treat yourself to a delicious dinner at Cantinho do Avillez (https://www.cantinhodoavillez.pt/en), a modern Portuguese restaurant owned by renowned chef José Avillez. The restaurant is a 10-minute walk from Galeria Presença.

21:00 - Evening stroll along Rua das Flores After dinner, take a leisurely evening stroll along Rua das Flores, a picturesque street filled with art galleries, boutiques, and street performers.

23:00 - Return to accommodation

**Day 2:**

08:00 - Breakfast at Pão Fofo Padaria Start your day with a tasty breakfast at Pão Fofo Padaria (https://www.facebook.com/paofufopadaria/), a charming bakery offering a variety of breads, pastries, and sandwiches.

09:30 - Lello Bookstore and Centro Português de Fotografia Visit the famous Lello Bookstore (https://www.livrarialello.pt/en_US/), one of the most beautiful bookstores in the world, known for its stunning architecture. Afterward, head to the nearby Centro Português de Fotografia (http://www.cpf.pt/), a photography museum housed in a former prison. Both sites are within walking distance of each other.

12:30 - Lunch at Tapabento Enjoy a delightful lunch at Tapabento (http://www.tapabento.com/), a cozy restaurant offering a mix of Portuguese and international tapas. Tapabento is a 10-minute walk from Centro Português de Fotografia.

14:00 - Street Art Tour Embark on a guided street art tour with Porto Street Art Tours (https://www.portostreetarttours.com/) to discover the city's vibrant street art scene and learn about the artists behind the murals.

18:00 - Galeria Municipal do Porto Visit Galeria Municipal do Porto (https://www.galeriamunicipaldoporto.pt/), a contemporary art gallery showcasing exhibitions by Portuguese and international artists. The gallery is a 15-minute walk from the end of the street art tour.

20:00 - Dinner at Flow Restaurant & Bar Enjoy a fusion of Mediterranean and Portuguese cuisine at Flow Restaurant & Bar (https://www.flowrestaurant.pt/), a stylish restaurant with a contemporary atmosphere. Flow is a 10-minute walk from Galeria Municipal do Porto.

22:00 - Maus Hábitos Cultural Centre End your day with a visit to Maus Hábitos (https://www.maushabitos.com/), a cultural center that hosts art exhibitions, live music, and other events. The center is a 15-minute walk from Flow Restaurant & Bar.

23:00 - Return to accommodation

**Day 3:**

08:00 - Breakfast at Mercador Café Start your day with breakfast at Mercador Café (https://www.facebook.com/mercadorcafe/), a cozy spot offering a variety of fresh pastries, sandwiches, and specialty coffee.

09:30 - Casa da Música Visit Casa da Música (https://www.casadamusica.com/), an iconic concert hall known for its striking architecture. Take a guided tour to learn about the building and its history. To get there, take the metro from Aliados to Casa da Música station.

12:00 - Lunch at Brick Clérigos Have lunch at Brick Clérigos (https://www.facebook.com/brickclerigos/), a laid-back restaurant offering delicious sandwiches and salads. The restaurant is a 20-minute walk or a short metro ride (take the metro from Casa da Música to Trindade station) from Casa da Música.

14:00 - Centro de Arte Oliva Head to Centro de Arte Oliva (https://www.centrodearteoliva.pt/), a contemporary art center located in a former industrial complex. The center features exhibitions by both national and international artists. To get there, take the train from São Bento station to Oliveira de Azeméis, and then take a taxi or bus to the art center.

18:30 - Return to Porto Take the train back to Porto from Oliveira de Azeméis station.

20:00 - Dinner at O Buraco Enjoy a traditional Portuguese dinner at O Buraco (https://www.facebook.com/RestauranteOBuraco/), a popular local restaurant offering affordable, hearty meals. The restaurant is a 10-minute walk from São Bento station.

22:00 - Concert at Passos Manuel End your day with a live music performance at Passos Manuel (https://www.facebook.com/PassosManuelPorto/), a vibrant cultural venue located just a 5-minute walk from O Buraco.

23:00 - Return to accommodation

**Day 4:**

08:00 - Breakfast at Molete Bread & Breakfast Start your day with breakfast at Molete Bread & Breakfast (https://www.facebook.com/moleteporto/), a modern café offering a variety of pastries, sandwiches, and coffee.

09:30 - Museu Nacional da Imprensa Visit the Museu Nacional da Imprensa (http://www.museudaimprensa.pt/), a museum dedicated to the history of printing and graphic arts. To get there, take bus line 401 from Bolhão.

12:00 - Lunch at Travessa Enjoy a leisurely lunch at Travessa (https://www.facebook.com/atravessarestaurante/), a quaint restaurant offering traditional Portuguese dishes. Travessa is a 15-minute walk from the printing museum.

14:00 - Guided Art Gallery Tour Join a guided art gallery tour with Porto Art Gallery Tours (https://portoartgallerytours.pt/) to explore some of the city's most innovative contemporary art spaces. The tour will take you through a selection of galleries showcasing cutting-edge works by both Portuguese and international artists.

18:00 - Jardins do Palácio de Cristal After the gallery tour, unwind in the beautiful Jardins do Palácio de Cristal (https://www.cm-porto.pt/en/crystal-palace-gardens), a tranquil park that offers stunning views of the Douro River and the city. The park is a 15-minute walk from the last gallery on the tour.

20:00 - Dinner at Pedro Lemos Indulge in a refined dinner at Pedro Lemos (https://www.pedrolemos.net/), an acclaimed restaurant serving innovative Portuguese cuisine. The restaurant is located in Foz do Douro, a 30-minute walk from Jardins do Palácio de Cristal or a short taxi/Uber ride.

22:00 - Mirajazz End your Porto cultural experience with a night of live jazz music at Mirajazz (https://www.facebook.com/mirajazzporto/), a cozy riverside venue with a stunning view of the Douro River. Mirajazz is a 20-minute walk or a short taxi/Uber ride from Pedro Lemos.

00:00 - Return to accommodation

This 4-day cultural exploration in Porto is packed with art, history, and music experiences, providing you with a diverse and unforgettable journey through the city's rich cultural landscape. Enjoy discovering the vibrant art scene and the beautiful sights that Porto has to offer.

# Romantic Porto: A 3-Day Getaway for Couples

**Day 1:**

08:00 - Breakfast at Majestic Café Start your romantic getaway with breakfast at the elegant Majestic Café (https://www.cafemajestic.com/en/), a historic Art Nouveau café known for its stunning decor and delicious pastries.

09:30 - Crystal Palace Gardens Take a leisurely morning stroll through the beautiful Jardins do Palácio de Cristal (https://www.cm-porto.pt/en/crystal-palace-gardens), a tranquil park that offers breathtaking views of the Douro River and the city.

11:00 - Livraria Lello Visit the enchanting Livraria Lello (https://www.livrarialello.pt/en_US/), one of the most beautiful bookstores in the world, known for its stunning architecture and intricate wooden staircase.

12:30 - Lunch at Cantina 32 Enjoy a delicious lunch at Cantina 32 (https://www.facebook.com/cantina32), a trendy restaurant offering contemporary Portuguese cuisine with a twist.

14:00 - Ribeira District Spend the afternoon exploring the picturesque Ribeira District, a UNESCO World Heritage Site with narrow streets, colorful houses, and charming squares.

16:30 - Douro River Cruise Embark on a romantic Douro River cruise with Rota do Douro (https://www.rotadodouro.pt/en), taking in the stunning scenery and enjoying a glass of Port wine as you sail past iconic landmarks.

19:00 - Dinner at DOP Indulge in a gourmet dinner at DOP (https://www.ruipaula.com/web/dop/), a sophisticated restaurant by acclaimed chef Rui Paula, offering a refined take on traditional Portuguese cuisine.

21:00 - Evening stroll along Avenida dos Aliados After dinner, take a leisurely evening stroll along Avenida dos Aliados, a grand boulevard lined with historic buildings and twinkling lights.

23:00 - Return to accommodation

**Day 2:**

08:00 - Breakfast at Moustache Coffee House Start your day with a cozy breakfast at Moustache Coffee House (https://www.facebook.com/moustache.coffee.house), a charming café offering a variety of pastries, sandwiches, and specialty coffee.

09:30 - Serralves Museum and Park Visit the Serralves Museum (https://www.serralves.pt/en/), a contemporary art museum featuring works by national and international artists. After exploring the museum, take a leisurely stroll through the beautiful Serralves Park, located on the same grounds.

13:00 - Lunch at ODE Porto Wine House Enjoy a leisurely lunch at ODE Porto Wine House (https://www.odeportowinehouse.com/), a stylish restaurant that offers a unique culinary experience focused on Portuguese cuisine and local wines.

15:00 - Foz do Douro Head to Foz do Douro, the charming seaside area of Porto, for a romantic walk along the beach and the waterfront promenade.

17:30 - Felgueiras Lighthouse Visit the iconic Felgueiras Lighthouse, a perfect spot to watch the sunset and take in the stunning views of the Atlantic Ocean.

20:00 - Dinner at The Yeatman Experience an unforgettable dinner at The Yeatman (https://www.the-yeatman-hotel.com/en/), a Michelin-starred restaurant with panoramic views of Porto and the Douro River.

23:00 - Return to accommodation

**Day 3:**

08:00 - Breakfast at Noshi Coffee Start your day with breakfast at Noshi Coffee (https://www.facebook.com/noshicoffee/), a modern café offering a variety of fresh pastries, sandwiches, and specialty coffee.

09:30 - Church of São Francisco Visit the Church of São Francisco (https://www.ordemsaofrancisco.pt/en/), a beautiful Gothic church with ornate Baroque interiors, known for its intricate wood carvings and gilded decorations. The church is a 15-minute walk from Noshi Coffee.

11:00 - Tram ride to Passeio Alegre Take a scenic ride on the historic Tram Line 1 from São Francisco Church to Passeio Alegre, a lovely garden square by the river.

12:30 - Lunch at Pedro Lemos Enjoy a leisurely lunch at Pedro Lemos (https://www.pedrolemos.net/), a Michelin-starred restaurant offering contemporary Portuguese cuisine in an intimate setting. The restaurant is a 15-minute walk from Passeio Alegre.

14:30 - Clérigos Tower Head to Clérigos Tower (https://www.torredosclerigos.pt/en/), a Porto landmark with a stunning panoramic view of the city. Climb the 225 steps to the top for an unforgettable experience. The tower is a 20-minute walk or a short tram ride (take Tram Line 22) from Pedro Lemos.

16:00 - Wine tasting at Cálem Cellars Discover the world of Port wine with a guided tour and tasting at Cálem Cellars (https://www.calem.pt/en/). Learn about the history and production of Port wine while enjoying some of the finest vintages. The cellars are a 25-minute walk or a short tram ride (take Tram Line 1) from Clérigos Tower.

18:30 - Relax at the hotel or accommodation Take some time to relax and freshen up at your hotel or accommodation before heading out for the evening.

20:30 - Dinner at VINUM Restaurant & Wine Bar Indulge in a delicious dinner at VINUM Restaurant & Wine Bar (https://www.vinumatgrahams.com/en/), a contemporary restaurant located in the historic Graham's Port Lodge, offering stunning views of Porto and the Douro River.

22:00 - Nighttime walk on Dom Luís I Bridge End your romantic getaway with a nighttime walk on the iconic Dom Luís I Bridge, taking in the breathtaking views of Porto illuminated against the night sky.

23:00 - Return to accommodation

# Family-Friendly Porto: A 5-Day Itinerary for Families with Kids

**Day 1:**

08:00 - Breakfast at Confeitaria do Bolhão Start your family adventure with breakfast at Confeitaria do Bolhão (https://www.facebook.com/ConfeitariaBolhao), a historic pastry shop known for its traditional Portuguese pastries.

09:30 - Livraria Lello and Clérigos Tower Visit the enchanting Livraria Lello (https://www.livrarialello.pt/en_US/), one of the most beautiful bookstores in the world, known for its stunning architecture. Then, head to Clérigos Tower (https://www.torredosclerigos.pt/en/) for a panoramic view of Porto. Both sites are within walking distance of each other.

12:00 - Lunch at Mercado Bom Sucesso Enjoy a casual lunch at Mercado Bom Sucesso (https://www.facebook.com/mercado.bomsucesso), a lively market offering a wide variety of food stalls to suit every taste.

14:00 - World of Discoveries Visit the interactive museum World of Discoveries (https://www.worldofdiscoveries.com/), where kids can learn about Portuguese explorers and their discoveries through hands-on exhibits and a boat ride.

17:00 - Ribeira District Explore the charming Ribeira District, a UNESCO World Heritage Site with narrow streets, colorful houses, and a lovely waterfront promenade.

19:00 - Dinner at Jimão Tapas e Vinhos Enjoy a family-friendly dinner at Jimão Tapas e Vinhos (https://www.facebook.com/JimaoTapaseVinhos/), a cozy restaurant offering a variety of delicious tapas that everyone will love.

21:00 - Return to accommodation

**Day 2:**

08:00 - Breakfast at Manteigaria Start your day with a tasty breakfast at Manteigaria (https://www.facebook.com/manteigaria.oficial/), a popular bakery known for its delicious pastéis de nata, a traditional Portuguese custard tart.

09:30 - Tram ride to Foz do Douro Take a scenic ride on the historic Tram Line 1 from São Francisco Church to Foz do Douro, a lovely seaside area of Porto.

11:00 - Sea Life Porto Visit Sea Life Porto (https://www.visitsealife.com/porto/en/), an aquarium where kids can get up close and personal with a variety of marine creatures, including sharks, rays, and sea turtles.

13:30 - Lunch at Casa de Pasto da Palmeira Have a leisurely lunch at Casa de Pasto da Palmeira (https://www.facebook.com/Casa-de-Pasto-da-Palmeira-139891549386554/), a family-friendly restaurant offering a mix of Portuguese and international dishes.

15:00 - Passeio Alegre Park and Felgueiras Lighthouse Spend the afternoon at Passeio Alegre Park, a beautiful garden by the river, perfect for kids to run around and play. Visit the nearby Felgueiras Lighthouse and enjoy the stunning views of the Atlantic Ocean.

18:30 - Return to Porto

20:00 - Dinner at MUU Steakhouse Treat the family to a delicious dinner at MUU Steakhouse (https://www.muu.pt/), a modern restaurant offering a variety of mouthwatering meat dishes and a kid-friendly menu.

22:00 - Return to accommodation

**Day 3:**

08:00 - Breakfast at Nata Lisboa Start your day with breakfast at Nata Lisboa (https://www.natalisboa.com/), a charming café offering a variety of fresh pastries, sandwiches, and coffee.

09:30 - Palácio de Cristal Gardens and Porto City Park Spend the morning exploring the beautiful Jardins do Palácio de Cristal (https://www.cm-porto.pt/en/crystal-palace-gardens), a tranquil park that offers breathtaking views of the Douro River and the city. Afterward, head to Porto City Park (https://www.cm-porto.pt/en/city-park), one of the largest urban parks in Portugal, perfect for picnics and outdoor activities.

12:30 - Lunch at Capa Negra II Enjoy a delicious lunch at Capa Negra II (https://www.facebook.com/Capa-Negra-II-221556294540332/), a traditional Portuguese restaurant offering a variety of family-friendly dishes.

14:00 - Serralves Museum and Park Visit the Serralves Museum (https://www.serralves.pt/en/), a contemporary art museum featuring works by national and international artists. After exploring the museum, take a leisurely stroll through the beautiful Serralves Park, located on the same grounds.

17:30 - Miniature Train Ride at Foz do Douro Head back to Foz do Douro and take the kids on a fun miniature train ride along the waterfront promenade.

19:00 - Dinner at Casa Guedes Have a tasty, casual dinner at Casa Guedes (https://www.facebook.com/CasaGuedes/), a popular local eatery known for its delicious pork sandwiches.

21:00 - Return to accommodation

**Day 4:**

08:00 - Breakfast at Molete Bread & Breakfast Start your day with breakfast at Molete Bread & Breakfast (https://www.facebook.com/moleteporto/), a modern café offering a variety of pastries, sandwiches, and coffee.

09:30 - Santo Inácio Zoo Spend the day at Santo Inácio Zoo (https://www.zoosantoinacio.com/en/), where the whole family can enjoy close encounters with a wide variety of animals, including lions, giraffes, and penguins.

13:00 - Lunch at the Zoo's Café Take a lunch break at the zoo's café, offering a selection of sandwiches, salads, and snacks.

14:30 - Continue exploring the zoo

17:30 - Return to Porto

19:00 - Dinner at Brasão Cervejaria Aliados Enjoy a hearty dinner at Brasão Cervejaria Aliados ([https://www.facebook.com/BrasaoCervejariaAliados/](https://www.facebook.com/BrasaoCervejariaAliados/)), a lively brewery and restaurant offering a variety of dishes and craft beers.

21:00 - Return to accommodation

**Day 5:**

08:00 - Breakfast at Mesa 325 Start your day with breakfast at Mesa 325 ([https://www.facebook.com/mesa325/](https://www.facebook.com/mesa325/)), a cozy café offering a variety of fresh pastries, sandwiches, and coffee.

09:30 - Matosinhos Beach Head to Matosinhos Beach for a day of sun and relaxation. The beach is perfect for families and offers a variety of water sports and activities.

13:00 - Lunch at O Valentim Enjoy a leisurely lunch at O Valentim ([https://www.facebook.com/Restaurante-O-Valentim-352742571465619/](https://www.facebook.com/Restaurante-O-Valentim-352742571465619/)), a popular seafood restaurant near the beach.

15:00 - Surfing Lessons If your kids are interested, sign up for a family surfing lesson with a local surf school.

18:30 - Return to Porto

20:00 - Farewell Dinner at Tapabento End your family trip with a delicious dinner at Tapabento ([https://www.tapabento.com/](https://www.tapabento.com/)), a trendy restaurant offering a variety of tapas and Portuguese cuisine. Don't forget to try their famous Francesinha, a delicious sandwich smothered in melted cheese and rich tomato sauce.

22:00 - Return to accommodation

**Day 6:**

08:00 - Breakfast at Café Santiago On your last morning, enjoy breakfast at Café Santiago ([https://www.cafesantiago.pt/](https://www.cafesantiago.pt/)), a traditional Portuguese café offering a wide selection of pastries, sandwiches, and coffee.

09:30 - Majestic Café and Bolhão Market Visit the iconic Majestic Café ([http://www.cafemajestic.com/](http://www.cafemajestic.com/)), a beautifully preserved café dating back to the 1920s. Afterward, head to Bolhão Market ([https://www.mercadobolhao.com/](https://www.mercadobolhao.com/)), a bustling local market where you can purchase fresh produce and souvenirs.

12:00 - Lunch at O Paparico Have a final lunch at O Paparico (https://www.opaparico.com/), an authentic Portuguese restaurant known for its delicious traditional dishes and warm atmosphere.

14:00 - São Bento Train Station Before leaving Porto, make sure to stop by São Bento Train Station (https://www.visitportugal.com/en/NR/exeres/3E423E3D-28C1-492C-ACB9-A2D1297E0226), famous for its stunning azulejo tiles that depict scenes from Portuguese history.

15:30 - Departure Head to the airport or train station for your departure, taking with you beautiful memories of your family-friendly Porto adventure. Safe travels!

# Thank You!

As you conclude your unforgettable trip to Porto, we hope you've had the chance to experience the unique charm, rich history, and vibrant culture that this enchanting city has to offer. From exploring iconic landmarks and stunning architecture to indulging in mouthwatering Portuguese cuisine, Porto is a true gem that leaves every visitor with lasting memories.

Thank you for choosing our travel guide to help you navigate your way through this incredible destination. We trust that the information, suggestions, and tips provided have enriched your experience and made your journey smoother and more enjoyable. As you continue to explore new places and embark on exciting adventures, remember to cherish the moments and make the most of every experience.

Safe travels and até breve, Porto!

Your friends at Guidora.

# Copyright Notice

**Guidora Porto in 3 Days Travel Guide ©**

## Disclaimer

The publishers have checked the information in this travel guide but its accuracy is not warranted or guaranteed. Tokyo visitors are advised that opening times should always be checked before making a journey.

## Tracing Copyright Owners

Every effort has been made to trace the copyright holders of referred material. Where these efforts have not been successful, copyright owners are invited to contact the editor (Guidora) so that their copyright can be acknowledged and/or the material removed from the publication.

## Creative Commons Content

We are most grateful to publishers of CreativeCommons material, including images. Our policies concerning this material are (1) to credit the copyright owner, and provide a link where possible  (2) to remove Creative Commons material, at once, if the copyright owner so requests - for example if the owner changes the licensing of an image.

We will also keep our interpretation of the Creative Commons Non-Commercial license under review. Along with, we believe, most web publishers, our current view is that acceptance of the 'Non-Commercial condition means (1) we must not sell the image or any publication containing the image (2) we may however use an image as an illustration for some information which is not being sold or offered for sale.

## Note to other copyright owners

We are grateful to those copyright owners who have given permission for their material to be used. Some of the material comes from secondary and tertiary sources. In every case we have tried to locate the original author or photographer and make the appropriate acknowledgement. In some cases the sources have proved obscure and we have been unable to track them down. In these cases, we would like to hear from the copyright owners and will be pleased to acknowledge them in future editions or remove the material.

Made in the USA
Las Vegas, NV
29 November 2023

81793775R00056